A MAGICAL FUSION OF GREEK & MIDDLE EASTERN VEGAN CUISINE

MIRIAM SORRELL

greenhouse publications

Enquiries please contact Jonathan Sorrell : jonsorrl@onvol.net
Published by Greenhouse Publications.

All food preparation, styling, design & photography : Miriam Sorrell
Layout, editing & proof-reading : Jonathan Sorrell
Cover design by Miriam Sorrell
Back cover and spine watermark design courtsey of Melazerg/Shutterstock.com
Image p. 150 "Bakdash ice-cream shop in the old souk in Damascus"
courtesy of Ankara, www. commons.wikimedia.org

ISBN : 978-99957-0-891-7

This book is dedicated to all animals in the world,
in particular long suffering ones,
and to the memory of my beloved Mikki

Contents

Introduction

My first book, *Mouthwatering Vegan*, embraced many of the cuisines close to my heart, and I would say that, together with my blog, it has already significantly changed the face of vegan food for many, since it was published almost three years ago. I have received a steady stream of mail from followers worldwide thanking me for the positive impact my recipes and cooking style have had on their lives, and on those of their families, vegan and non-vegan alike.

Let's start from here. It is not easy, even with today's increased variety and availability of plant-based foods, to adopt a vegan diet. Many factors come into play – time to prepare food, working out a compromise plan for all the family (bearing in mind they may not all be vegan), and generally being ready to take the plunge into an exciting new cuisine with its complexities and differences. So my contribution has been to create and formulate recipes that combine the fundamental plusses that make for delicious accessible meals.

In the past, I have adapted/veganized a number of well-known favourites, maintaining the essence of the original recipe, whilst replacing meat and dairy ingredients with my plant-based alternatives – encompassing Italian pasta dishes, English breakfast (including 'bangers' and even fried eggs), Indian curries, numerous burgers, classic desserts, cheeses, milks, eggs, and so forth. Then, along with these staples, I have created many of my own original dishes, and have also introduced people to less well-known foods from more exotic lands (bearing in mind my own bloodline – Greek, Greek Cypriot, etc.) – Israeli *shakshuka*, Greek *pastitsio*, Lebanese *labneh*, and so on. In the main, this has worked very well, judging from the feedback I receive. I suppose all this reflects my own cultural heritage and my passionate desire to expand the horizons, raise the bar, and bring all this wondrous sensuality to the vegan table. I have enjoyed a huge life benefit by being vegan – but my primary reason and focus has always been to see a radically better life for our fellow sentient beings on this planet. So this biting ethical belief is my driving force, together with my own need for artistic self-expression. I love to create – I am a painter and designer, and through my food writing, I have also become a pretty proficient photographer. I don't bang on about the non-purity of other vegans – I am a pragmatist,

I love life, and I don't see for one minute why choosing a vegan lifestyle should automatically make one a paid-up member of the 'Self-Sacrifice Club' !

The priorities in my cooking are very clear – I want the food to look as good as it tastes, I want the aroma to waft round the house, and I want to see many people cooking my food (it's incidental that it's vegan), having the time of their lives enjoying and celebrating with their friends and family. I strongly believe that main mealtimes should still be the heart of the day – when the shared pleasure of the food serves as a backdrop for everyone to wind down and indulge in catching up together, remembering that we are not simply on this planet to work and that eating should be much more than simply refueling !

And so to '*YASOU*'. "Why Middle Eastern cuisine ?", you may ask. Well, funnily enough, my more than passing fascination with the exotic, sensual, almost erotic nature of Middle Eastern food dates back to my early adulthood when I first entered the Spice Market in Istanbul, and was able to take in the breathtaking waft of the spices, and the wondrous splash of contrasting colours and textures, all accompanied by the constant hustle and bustle of the vendors and customers alike, as deals were struck, with happy faces all round. I have also been increasingly interested by my own hybrid linage, knowing that there was a pretty unusual range of bloods within the family tree. My father – who owned several restaurants in London - is pure Greek Cypriot, whereas my mother's history was far more complex. Born in Romania, her family were from Athens, with Maltese and Italian ancestry, her parents having also spent some time in Constantinople. Although I was born in cosmopolitan London, I had always considered myself broadly Mediterranean, until I recently considered the fact that Cyprus is part Mediterranean, part Middle Eastern – hardly surprising given that it lies south of Turkey, and north of Egypt. So, I guess at a push I could add a smattering of Persian to my roots.

This may well have contributed to the love affair I am presently enjoying with the foods from this region. I am also finding it to be so interesting and inspiring when I discover the parallels existing within cuisines from different (though often neighbouring) cultures, where traditional dishes (or even staples) from one are adapted by another. Names often remain similar – for example, the Persian *kufta* is the Indian/Pakistani *kofta*, or the Greek *keftés*, each derived from one another, but lending themselves to very different cuisines. I am just so enthralled and inspired by the depth of history, the richness of culture, and yet the very real connection these foods have with the pulse and bloodline of these extraordinary nations. I view the traditional recipes of countries such as Iran, Turkey, Israel, Lebanon, to name but a few, with a heightened sense of reverence – as though I have been honoured in being allowed access to recreate them myself. I have had such fun and joy in working my own vegan creations, being inspired by what I have tasted, seen, and read, and in so doing, completely immersing myself in the process of cooking what I consider to be some of the best vegan food I have ever tasted. Then add in a touch of Mediterranean - inevitable since I have spent most of my life living in the south of this region - and you have *Yasou*!

Where *Mouthwatering Vegan* served to demonstrate that there are virtually no boundaries when it comes to vegan cooking, this book comes from a special place within, and defines Me - where I've come from, and where I'd like to spend more time. This is real food from the heart – not pretentious or contrived, not designed to fit a particular style or fashion, or manufactured to satisfy a particular dietary fad – it's food that proudly exists in its own right, and it also happens to be vegan – though I've never seen that as limiting. As a result of my own multi-cultural background I've been enormously privileged to have had access to such a diverse array of exotic foods – from the simplest snack eaten by the seaside to the most lavish courses prepared for dinner parties. I've also witnessed the ever-increasing diversity of cuisines becoming available to us all, and a public that embraces this cultural diversity, thanks partly to brilliant marketing and to our superb worldwide communications networks. Today, if you walk into a main branch of any of the large supermarket chains, you'll find practically any food you're looking for, and most likely take it for granted. But remember, this would have been inconceivable a decade or two ago. I am hugely excited and inspired by this, and I always buy and try new ingredients I've not seen before, introducing them into my own pantry. In fact, I have always loved the fusion of unlikelies, and I'm a great believer in mixed marriages at the table ! In this next book I want to pay homage to my own roots, but err more towards the exotic Middle Eastern cuisine, which also happens to be in tune with an increased proliferation of Arabic and Middle Eastern restaurants and foodstuffs available in the Western world.

I hope that through my efforts, I will bring a further dimension to those wishing to explore and indulge in some of the most exotic, beautiful, passionate, and sensual food in the world, and whilst doing so, be comfortably reassured in the knowledge that they are not harming animals, are doing far less harm to themselves, and are working towards the long-term good of our planet. We are a growing community brought together by this shared love of our planet, and a sense of moral responsibility to watch over and protect its more vulnerable inhabitants.

On our journey we come across many painful and disturbing images, which cause us a great deal of suffering and distress, and many a time this can also leave us in a state of enormous frustration as we face the daily challenge of trying to enlighten the blind in this respect, and achieve the seemingly impossible task of getting the rest of the world to understand their inherent wrongdoings. It can be a very isolating and lonely space to be in, and it also causes many of us to become incensed and angry. This anger needs to be vented and channeled, and it's so easy to misdirect it, and take it out on one another. So, with mindful and heartfelt awareness, let's always try to transcend our differences, look beyond our petty squabbles and bickering on Facebook (which only serve to delight our critics), and celebrate together in indulging in this Food for the Gods ! What better way to use up that pent up energy than getting creative in the kitchen ? Though I have to say, another force drives me when I cook - I am no longer Miriam the activist, but Miriam the alchemist. Truly, because I can see and taste the result before I cook. Then once I'm in the kitchen, I am so engrossed in my cooking, that the experience is almost meditative. I can define this as a true state of joy and contentment. That's not to say that putting this book together was an effortless breeze. I have been working many months, years in fact, including many sleepless nights, to create this collection - but it's still been a labour of love in the literal sense.

I have a strong affinity with the sensuality of the ingredients I use - their colours and aromas, their textures, tastes and shapes - combining them to enjoy their magic, and transforming them into my own unique and memorable dishes - creating a happy table, warm hearts, enchanted spirits, smiles and voracious appetites for all that this good earth is happy to offer. And I like to put these offerings forward, playing my role as your recipe host, from my kitchen to yours with love.

Miriam Sorrell
February 2016

Vegan Pantry

There are a number of basics and vegan essentials you should have in your kitchen before you begin. Below are some of the tools, ingredients and supplies you'll need.

Kitchen Equipment

Food processor

A good-quality, powerful food processor is essential for a variety of kitchen tasks, including puréeing, chopping, shredding, grinding and mixing. KitchenAid, Cuisinart and Magimix are excellent brands.

Blender

You'll need a powerful standing blender, such as a VitaMix or KitchenAid, for blending smoothies and chopping hard ingredients like nuts. This is an item where it really pays to invest in quality, as the difference a high-powered blender makes is remarkable.

Handheld immersion blender

A handheld blender is useful for puréeing soups and sauces without having to transfer them from their container.

Juicer

A high-capacity juicer lets you enjoy the myriad benefits of fresh, raw juices. You can put most fruits and vegetables in whole, though citrus fruits need to be peeled first.

Ice-cream maker

You can buy commercial vegan ice creams and sorbets, but it's more fun to make your own. It's not necessary to buy an expensive ice-cream maker—a cheap one will do the job.

Pudding basin

Some of my desserts call for pudding basins, stoneware bowls that come in various sizes. They are inexpensive and available in kitchen stores.

Kitchen Scales

A small set of kitchen scales is helpful for weighing precise amounts of ingredients such as tofu (when a recipe calls for less than a full package), chocolate or nuts. You can find inexpensive models—either a digital or analog scale will do.

Greaseproof / Parchment paper

Greaseproof paper (parchment paper) is useful for lining baking pans; I also use it in my no-bake dessert recipes to avoid sticking and to prevent pans from getting scratched.

Vegan Dairy

Milk

Commercial nondairy milks come in many flavours and varieties, including soymilk, rice milk, oat milk, coconut milk and nut milk. Different brands vary in thickness, sweetness and taste, so sample a variety to find your preference. Or try making your own (see the recipe for Happy Milk on page 249 of my 'Mouthwatering Vegan' cookbook).

Margarine

Not all brands of margarine are vegan—some contain dairy products—so be sure to read the ingredients. Earth Balance brand is vegan, non-hydrogenated and all natural, and also comes in a soy-free version. Some types of margarine are not suitable for baking, so check the label.

Cheese

For cheese alternatives, see the recipes on pages 252-262 of the Decadent Cheeses & Dairy Alternatives chapter in my 'Mouthwatering Vegan' cookbook, or look for Daiya, Galaxy, Sheese, or Tofutti brands in stores. Some nondairy cheeses contain casein, a milk protein, so check the label to make sure it's vegan.
For a grated hard cheese alternative, you may be able to find packaged grated vegan "Parmesan" alternatives made from soy (look for Parmazano or Galaxy brands) or nuts (Parma! or Parma-Veg), or try my Nutty Parmesan recipe on page 262 of my 'Mouthwatering Vegan' cookbook.
I hope my own MIDAS brand should be available before too long in shops in the UK and Europe, although it is a lengthy and complex process bringing a new food brand to the market. www.midasdeli.com.

Cream cheese

Tofutti and Galaxy brands make vegan cream cheese, available in tubs in the refrigerator section of natural food stores and some supermarkets. It comes in several flavours (plain, French onion, garlic and herb, etc.) and can be used as a spread or in cooking and baking.

Cream

Many of my recipes call for vegan cream. MimicCreme, a dairy- and soy-free cream substitute made from nuts, is available in some natural food stores, and comes in sweetened and unsweetened versions. You can also make an easy cashew cream that substitutes well for cream in any recipe (see the recipe for Happy Cream on page 249 of my 'Mouthwatering Vegan' cookbook).

Yoghurt

Yoghurt made from cultured soy, coconut or almond milk is available in dairy sections in a variety of flavours. Use plain soy yogurt for the most neutral flavour in recipes.

Grains

I prefer to cook with whole grains, as they contain much more fibre and minerals than refined versions. Among the ones to have on hand are brown rice (short-grain, long-grain and basmati), wild rice, quinoa, barley, millet and rolled oats. In some dishes, where the texture of white rice is preferable, I use short-grain or long-grain white rice, or arborio rice. These grains are all available in packages or bulk bins in health shops, natural food stores and supermarkets.

To cook perfectly fluffy grains, I like to use more water than necessary, then drain and rinse the cooked grain (much like cooking pasta). Here is the basic recipe: Combine 1 cup (250 mL) grain with 3 cups (750 mL) water in a saucepan. Bring to a boil, cover, reduce the heat and simmer until tender (anywhere from 15 to 60 minutes, depending on the type of grain). Drain and rinse in cold water before adding to your recipe.

Flours

I use wholewheat flour wherever possible, though where a recipe needs a more refined texture, unbleached all-purpose flour is best. Flours made from brown rice and spelt (a variety of wheat that is often well tolerated by people with wheat allergies) are also good to have on hand. Chickpea flour (sometimes called gram flour), made from ground chickpeas, makes a good binder in burger and sausage recipes. Soy flour, also found in health and natural food stores, adds protein and moistness to eggless baked goods. Self-raising (or self-rising) flour is cake or pastry flour that already has baking powder added; you can substitute 1 cup (250 mL) regular all- purpose flour plus 1½ tsp (7 .5 mL) baking powder plus ¼ tsp (1 mL) salt for 1 cup (250 mL) of self- raising flour.

Beans

Dried beans are inexpensive and easy to prepare, as long as you plan ahead. Some of my favourite varieties are red and brown lentils (which need no presoaking), split peas, pinto beans and fava beans. Most of my recipes use tinned beans: red kidney beans, cannellini (white kidney) beans, chickpeas, lentils and vegan baked beans (check the ingredients, as some tinned baked beans include pork). Drain and rinse tinned beans before using to reduce the sodium content.

Pasta

Some dried pasta contains eggs, but many varieties are vegan—read the ingredients. I like to use wholewheat pasta wherever possible, but there are many other kinds available; if you're gluten-intolerant, try quinoa or brown rice noodles, though there are a number of gluten-free brands of pasta available now. Fresh pasta almost always contains eggs, but it is possible to find vegan ravioli or other shapes from specialty pasta makers.

Tofu and Meat Substitutes

There are many commercially available meat substitutes, but be aware that not all are vegan, as some contain egg whites or dairy products. My personal favorites come from the Linda McCartney range, but I would also recommend Gardein, Yves Veggie, Lightlife and Smart Menu brands as alternatives. Quorn is now finally introducing a vegan range (up until now, they have used egg white as a binder in virtually all of their products) - I have personally campaigned for this exciting development.

Tofu

Tofu is a versatile food that can be used for many different dishes, including scrambled tofu, stir-fries, cheesecake and more. The kind I use most often is firm silken tofu, which blends smoothly for sauces and desserts. Look for Mori-Nu (which comes in Tetra Paks and does not require refrigeration) or Nasoya brands in natural food stores and some supermarkets. You can substitute firm regular tofu in recipes where it is not blended.

Textured vegetable protein (TVP)

Textured vegetable protein, or TVP, is made from defatted soy flour. It is sold dried and can usually be found as granules (to substitute for ground meat in Bolognese sauce, chili, etc.) or as chunks suitable for stews. It must be hydrated before being added to recipes. To hydrate, combine TVP with an equal amount (or slightly less) of hot water or broth in a bowl, and let stand for 5 minutes (it will approximately double in volume). You can also add soy sauce, spices, or other seasonings to the TVP; much like tofu, it will readily absorb the flavours of anything you add to it.

Vegan mince meat (ground meat) substitutes
You can find vegan mince meat substitutes, usually made from soy, in the refrigerator section of most supermarkets and grocery stores. They work well in place of minced beef in many recipes, such as shepherd's pie and Bolognese sauce. You can also substitute crumbled or chopped veggie burgers, or chopped pecans.

Bacon
Some substitutes contain egg white. Look for vegan varieties from Lightlife or Yves Veggie.

Vegan burgers
There are many varieties of premade vegan burgers, which can usually be found refrigerated or frozen. Some are more "meatlike," while others contain a mixture of grains, nuts or vegetables. Again, many varieties of vegetarian burgers contain eggs or dairy, so read the labels.

Vegan "beef" strips
You can find these in the refrigerator or freezer section of natural food stores and regular grocery stores. They are useful in stews—Gardein and Yves Veggie brands are the best known. If you're avoiding soy, you can substitute seitan (wheat gluten) strips.

Nuts and Seeds

Nuts and seeds are an excellent vegan source of protein, minerals and healthy fats, and are important ingredients in many of my recipes. I like to use walnuts, pecans, hazelnuts, pistachios, cashews, almonds, shredded coconut and sunflower seeds.
To toast raw nuts, place them in a dry frying pan over medium–high heat for a few minutes, stirring often, until they're golden brown; alternatively, spread them in a single layer on a baking sheet and roast in a 350oF (180oC) oven for 10–15 minutes, checking frequently so they don't get overbrowned.

Oils

Extra virgin olive oil
Olive oil is my standby for sautéing, frying, drizzling, and salad dressings.

Sunflower oil
I use this light oil for baking, or wherever a more neutral flavour is desired, but you could substitute any other light-tasting oil, such as canola or grapeseed oil.

Sesame oil
This oil, which comes in light and dark (toasted) varieties, adds a nutty flavour to Asian dishes, and works well in stir-fries and Thai curries. Light sesame oil has a higher smoke point than dark, so it is more suitable for deep-frying.

Unsweetened coconut oil
This amazing oil, which is semisolid at room temperature, is excellent for frying, and works well in desserts. The saturated fat it contains has incredible health benefits, unlike the saturated fat found in animal products. Please look for a fair trade, cruelty-free brand.

Flaxseed oil
Flaxseed oil is high in omega-3 fatty acids and makes a great addition to salad dressings and dips. It should not be heated or used for frying, as this alters its chemical composition.

Herbs and Spices

I like to cook with a variety of herbs, spices and seasonings. Here are the essentials to have on hand:

- sea salt or Himalayan salt
- coriander (seeds and ground)
- fresh coriander /cilantro
- cardamom (seeds and ground)
- cumin (seeds and ground)
- fennel seeds
- turmeric
- curry powder (regular, hot and mild)
- garam masala
- paprika (regular, smoked and sweet)
- crushed red chili pepper flakes
- chili powder
- panch puren (a blend of cumin, fennel, fenugreek, brown mustard seed and kalonji)
- fresh chilies
- parsley (fresh and dried)
- basil (fresh and dried)
- dried oregano
- dried thyme
- ground cinnamon
- ground nutmeg
- ground allspice
- pumpkin pie spice
- onion powder
- garlic granules and powder
- lemongrass
- fresh ginger
- ground sumac (available in Middle Eastern grocery stores)
- whole peppercorns
- Chinese five-spice powder
- asafoetida powder (available in Indian grocery stores)
- za'atar (buy the dried herb mix – usually contains thyme, oregano and marjoram, and sometimes sumac and salt)
- isot pepper (also known as Urfa biber) is a dried Turkish chili pepper. It is often described as having a smoky, 'raisin-like' taste.

Binders

Arrowroot powder and cornstarch

Arrowroot (a white powder made from a starchy tuber) and cornstarch can often be used interchangeably for thickening sauces, gravies, puddings and more. Cornstarch turns liquid opaque when mixed, so arrowroot is better suited to clear jellies and sauces.

Agar flakes & powder

Agar is a type of seaweed that is used as a thickener and stabilizer. It is available in both powder and flake forms from natural food stores. I use agar powder in some my earlier cheese recipes (pages 252-262 of my 'Mouthwatering Vegan' cookbook).

It can also be used to make vegan Jell-O–type desserts, in place of gelatin (which is derived from animal bones): dissolve 1–2 Tbsp (15–30 mL) of agar flakes in 1 cup (250 mL) of fruit juice, simmer until slightly thickened and then chill until set.

Flaxseed

Flaxseed is very high in fiber and omega-3 fatty acids. Ground flaxseed is preferable, as whole flaxseeds tend to pass through the body undigested; you can purchase it ground, or grind whole flaxseeds yourself in a coffee grinder or food processor. Flaxseed can be used as a binder to replace eggs in baking: to replace 1 egg, mix 1 Tbsp (15 mL) ground flaxseed with 3 Tbsp (45 mL) water.

Egg replacer powder

A combination of starches that mimics the leavening and binding properties of eggs in baking. Orgran and Ener-G brands can be found in natural food stores.

Sweeteners

Sugar

Although granulated white sugars in Europe are generally vegan, some brands of refined white sugar and icing sugar sold in North America are not, as cane sugars are often processed using animal bone char (some are not, but it's impossible to tell without contacting the manufacturer). Brown sugar—which is really refined white sugar with added molasses—may also be processed in this way. Try to buy organic sugar, unbleached sugar, raw cane sugar (also called turbinado sugar) or Sucanat (evaporated cane juice). Wholesome Sweeteners and Whole Foods' 365 label are brands to look for. Muscovado sugar is a dark brown sugar with a strong molasses flavour—you can substitute dark brown sugar. Stevia and xylitol are good natural sugar substitutes.

Agave and maple syrup

Agave and maple syrup are the liquid sweeteners I use most often. Agave syrup, or nectar, is a low-glycemic natural sweetener extracted from the agave plant, ideal as an all-purpose sweetener and for sweetening drinks, as it dissolves well. Maple syrup, from the sap of the maple tree, is another natural vegan sweetener prized for its unique flavour. They can often be used interchangeably, or in place of honey. You can also substitute brown rice syrup, barley malt syrup or date syrup, all available from natural food stores.

Flavourings

Nutritional yeast

Nutritional yeast is high in vitamin B12, usually found in animal products, making it an important source for vegans of this essential nutrient. The yeast is deactivated, so it's not suitable for baking. The bright yellow flakes have a nutty, cheesy flavour, which makes them an excellent addition to vegan cheese sauces, pastas, scrambled tofu and more. You can find nutritional yeast in bulk in health shops and natural food stores.

Vinegar

Vinegar adds tanginess and depth of flavour to food. For salad dressings and seasoning, I use balsamic vinegar or apple cider vinegar. Rice vinegar is good for Asian dishes.

HP Sauce

HP Sauce, or brown sauce, is a traditional condiment made from malt vinegar, tomato, dates, tamarind and spices. It contains no animal ingredients.

Miso

A fermented paste made from soybeans, often combined with rice or other grains, miso is a salty, savory and protein-rich addition to soups, sauces and other dishes. You can buy miso, which comes in varieties ranging from light to dark, in Asian or natural food stores. I prefer the dark variety, which has a richer flavour.

Soy sauce/tamari

Tamari is a naturally fermented soy sauce that adds a deep, complex flavour to many vegan dishes. You can use it interchangeably with regular soy sauce, which is slightly saltier.

Gluten- free tamari is also available. Look for tamari in natural food stores or supermarkets.

Teriyaki sauce

A sweet, savory, soy-based sauce used in Asian dishes. I like to make my own, but you can also use a bottled version.

Vegetable stock

Vegetable stock can be purchased as granules, powder or cubes, and adds flavour to soups and sauces. I prefer granules, as they distribute better, but powder or cubes can be substituted. Better Than Bouillon brand produces a vegetarian chicken- flavoured stock, useful for "chicken" noodle soup.

Curry paste

For Indian-style curries, I often use tikka or tandoori curry pastes, which are combinations of various Indian spices with oil and other ingredients. Patak's brand is available in Asian stores and in the ethnic food aisles of most supermarkets.

Tahini

Tahini, a paste made from ground sesame seeds, is high in protein and calcium and adds creaminess to dips, dressings and other dishes. You can find it in most grocery stores.

Yeast extract

Marmite and Vegemite are the best-known brands of yeast extract, a salty, slightly bitter black paste that comes in jars and tubes. Some people like it spread on toast, and a little bit adds saltiness and depth of flavour to savory dishes. You'll find it in natural food stores and and in supermarkets.

Sweet chili sauce

Sweet chili sauce is made from chilies and a sweetener. It's a popular condiment in Asian cooking and can be found in Asian grocery stores, and in the ethnic food aisles in supermarkets.

Worcestershire sauce

Worcestershire sauce often contains anchovies, so look for vegetarian varieties in health shops and natural food stores. In the US you can find Annie's Naturals Organic Vegan Worcestershire Sauce at www.veganessentials.com, and Henderson's Relish is sold through Amazon UK, and is said to be good, though I haven't tried it myself.

Rosewater, rose essence, rose syrup and rose petals

These add a lovely floral flavour to desserts and savory dishes. You can find rose water and rose essence (also called rose extract) in health shops and natural food stores, or natural pharmacies; the essence is much more concentrated. Rose syrup, which is sweetened, is usually available in Indian, Middle Eastern, and Asian grocery stores and in some supermarkets. For fresh rose petals, look for unsprayed roses at farmers' markets or through organic florists. Edible dried rose petals are available in some gourmet food stores and Middle Eastern grocery stores, or find them online through Amazon.com or eBay.

Vegan jelly

Most jelly is made from gelatin, an animal product. For a vegan alternative, try Just Wholefoods Real Fruit brand, available in some natural food stores and through online vegan specialty stores. You can also substitute agar flakes or agar powder.

Pastry

Puff pastry

Puff pastry is a layered pastry for making light, flaky pie crusts. I find it's too time-consuming to make my own, so I prefer to use a good- quality ready-made brand, such as Aussie Bakery (available at Whole Foods), Pepperidge Farm, or Jus Rol in the UK and Europe.

Filo / Phyllo pastry

Made from very thin sheets of dough, filo is used in Greek and Middle Eastern pastries, such as baklava. Many brands of filo dough are vegan (check the ingredients), and whole wheat and spelt filo sheets are also available.

Where to Buy

Depending on where you live, some vegan ingredients can be difficult to find in grocery stores. Here are some online retailers that can help you stock your pantry with vegan essentials and hard-to-find ingredients, including baking supplies, dairy, meat and egg substitutes, and more.

- Karmavore: www.karmavore.ca - ships worldwide
- Vegan Essentials: www.veganessentials.com - ships worldwide
- The Vegan Store: www.veganstore.com - ships within the U.S. and Canada
- Viva Vegan Store: www.vivavegan.ca - ships to Canada and the continental U.S.
- Whole Foods Market: www.wholefoodsmarket.com - online shopping available in some areas; check site for details.
- Holland & Barrett: www.hollandandbarrett.com/ deliver throughout the UK
- Goodness Direct : www.goodnessdirect.co.uk ship to nearly all destinations within the UK, and non-chilled to selected countries outside the UK

Important Note regarding meat & dairy alternatives for readers of this book :

Kindly note that those of us who are vegan are all different, and we ought to accept our differences with grace and respect. If some of you may not like the idea of faux meat, then please substitute it with the French puy lentils (google where they are sold), and precook them according to the instructions. I love puy lentils because they have a chewy texture, and are befitting in many recipes that would otherwise call for a faux/fake/substitute for meat. In the same way as dairy milk is substituted with many types of non-dairy milk, from soya, to rice, oat, hemp, cashew, coconut and almond etc, so it's the same with cheese. There is no crime in recreating non-dairy cruelty-free versions of any of these, so long as the result is satisfying and ethical, and no animals are hurt or abused in any way in the making of them.

Note :

I have always been reluctant and cauious to suggest the number of portions a recipe will serve, since this depends upon people's appetite, and personal preference, Therefore the suggested number of portions are there as a rough guide.

DIPS, SALADS, SOUPS & SIDES

opposite page Fried Vegan Haloumi

SERVES 4

Beautiful Baba Ganoush

Here is one of the most delicious Baba Ganoush's I have ever tasted. Enjoyed with smoked hot pita bread and a drizzle of olive oil, it is in itself a hearty and rich appetizer. The flavours that merge from this little creation collide on your palette to bring you culinary joy and a wonderful smooth, rich texture, which makes it all the more moreish. Middle Eastern cuisine at its super best !

---

1 large aubergine/eggplant
½ tsp cumin seeds
1 to 2 cloves garlic, chopped
3 Tbsp fresh coriander/cilantro, chopped
1 Tbsp freshly chopped mint
salt to taste (don't omit this)
juice of ½ lemon (I use a tad more, as I like it tangy)
2 to 3 Tbsp (30 to 45 ml) olive oil
1 Tsp tahini

First, pierce holes around your aubergine with a sharp pointed knife. Next, using a toast fork or metal barbeque skewer, hold the aubergine over an open flame, and scorch it whilst turning it around a few times. Be patient - this is the only part of the process that takes some minutes to complete. When the aubergine wrinkles, it will produce a slightly burnt smell, more like a semi-pleasant 'smoked' smell. It is this smell that the aubergine will absorb, which gives it its magical smoked flavour. When the aubergine is done, place it on a plate and allow it to cool down for about 15 minutes. Then peel it, and place the flesh in a separate bowl. Meanwhile, dry-fry your cumin seeds in a non-stick pan for a couple of minutes, stirring all the time, then remove.

Next, place the remaining ingredients (except for the tahini and the liquids) in your food processor, and process for a minute, until all is finely chopped.

Now add the aubergine flesh, and process briefly for around 20 seconds. Then add the oil, lemon juice, and tahini, and process for an extra 20 seconds. Taste for salt and lemon.

Decant into a bowl and serve. Don't serve this too cold, as you then lose some of the flavour.

SERVES 4

Muhammara

Muhammara is the most delicious hot red pepper dip, and is most commonly found in Syrian, Levantine, and Turkish cuisines. I have mastered my version over the last few years, and have found just the right combination. The heat, sweet yet pungent taste, and all the different textures, both smooth and grainy, make this one of the most wonderful spreads in the world.

---

3 red Romano peppers (use bell peppers if you can't find Romano)
¾ cup brown bread crumbs, processed
1 cup walnuts
sea salt to taste
1½ tsp ground cumin
1 clove garlic, processed
2 baby chillies, de-seeded
1 Tbsp (15 ml) lemon juice
2 Tbsp (30 ml) olive oil
2 Tbsp (30 ml) pomegranate molasses syrup
a pinch of molasses (optional)

First, preheat your oven to 400ºF (200ºC).

Place your Romano peppers on a pre-greased oven tray, and bake until a little scorched. Remove from oven, allow to cool a little, before peeling and deseeding them and placing on a plate.

Process your breadcrumbs, and set aside. Then process your nuts slightly, as though you had chopped them with a knife, and place in a medium sized bowl.

Add your breadcrumbs on top of the chopped walnuts, followed by the salt and cumin, and stir with a spoon.

Now process the garlic in your food processor until very small, then add your chilli peppers, and whizz again. Add the cooked peppers, whizz again, then add the lemon juice, olive oil, pomegranate molasses syrup, and molasses, if needed. Now fold this mixture into the dried ingredients in the bowl, and stir well with a fork.

Spoon into a serving dish and serve. Alternatively, refrigerate, but be sure to take it out half an hour before eating, as I wouldn't suggest serving this cold.

SERVES 4

Vegan Taramasalata

Taramasalata is a very popular starter dip in Greece and Turkey, and enormously popular in other countries around the world. It is made from cured cod roe, and although that may not sound particularly appetizing, particularly amongst vegans, I admit it was a recipe I vowed I would veganize. This was a challenge to achieve, but the result is a sublime tasting, incredibly mouthwatering vegan taramasalata you will make for the rest of your life !

---

3 slices of slightly stale white bread (or ½ cup quiona)
1 tin precooked chickpeas (265g net)
½ red onion, chopped
2 Tbsp of vegan 'Fish' sauce (see recipe below)
½ tsp beetroot powder
the juice of 1 large lemon
Himalayan or sea salt to taste
around 100ml olive oil

You will need to have your vegan fish sauce already prepared, if you're making your own. You may wish to purchase a ready sauce – if so, be sure to check it is actually vegan.

First, process the bread in your processor, remove and set aside.

Next, place the chickpeas and the onion in a food processor, and process until smooth. Then add the remaining ingredients except for the bread and oil, process again, and add the oil a little at a time until you have a smooth texture. Finally add the breadcrumbs in at the end, and process for a few more seconds.

Spoon into container and refrigerate. Drizzle on some oil, and enjoy with hot pita bread or crudités of your choice.

'Fish' Sauce

¾ cup (188 ml) water
1 Tbsp (15 ml) agave syrup
½ cup (125 ml) soy sauce
1 tsp sea salt
2 tsp wakame powder
2 tsp kelp powder
1 tsp light brown miso
¼ cup black olive brine water (optional)

First, pulverize your wakame into a powder in your food processor. Empty your processor, measure out one tablespoon, and place back in your processor together with the rest of your ingredients. Process on low speed for 10 seconds - just long enough to integrate all the ingredients. Then store in a airtight jar or bottle, and refrigerate. The mixture should last for 1 to 2 months.

SERVES 4

Beetroot & Yoghurt Dip (Pancar Ezmesi)

This is a popular Turkish dip, that is healthy, low in fat, and completely delicious. Very simple to make, and I suggest serving with warm pita bread and crudités, or as part of a mezze course.

400g cooked beetroot
2 Tbsp (30 ml) olive oil
salt
1 tsp cumin powder
90 ml vegan yoghurt (see pg 65 for my Thick Vegan Greek Yoghurt)
2 cloves garlic, crushed

First, process the beetroot in your blender until broken down. Then add the remaining ingredients, and process until smooth. Refrigerate for at least a couple of hours before serving.

SERVES 4

Rich Spicy Bean Dip

This dip is full of Middle Eastern inspired flavours, with chilli, za'atar and other spices, lemon, and sun dried tomatoes - it's also very nutritious. The borlotti bean is a variety of cranberry bean, but with a thicker skin. Enjoy this dip with warm pita bread, with crudités, on toast, in a baguette, or as a sandwich filler. Warning - it's highly addictive !

---

1 400g (250g net) tin of fagioli borlotti (borlotti beans)
2 shallots, roughly chopped
½ clove garlic
1/8 tsp ground coriander/cilantro
¼ tsp za'atar
a pinch of cumin
¼ tsp chili powder
¼ tsp smoked paprika
¼ cup (63 ml) olive oil
6 sundried tomato halves
½ tsp sea salt
2 slices of brown bread (crusts removed)
1 tsp agave syrup
¼ cup fresh red bell pepper (capsicum), chopped
the juice of a large lemon
2 Tbsp fresh basil leaves, or fresh coriander/cilantro

Start off by blending the beans, then add the shallots and garlic, and process again. Now add the herbs (except for the basil) and spices, followed by the remaining ingredients (again except for the basil), and blend until smooth. Then finally add the basil, and blitz until the basil is only in specs, but still visible.

Decant, and drizzle in olive oil – cover, and refrigerate. Serve as per above suggestions.

SERVES 4

Ful Medames & Sun Dried Tomato Dip

Bigilla is a traditional Maltese dip - but it lacks something, I feel. Ful Medames (fava beans) are the beans used to make this dense dip, which is great with any Med or Middle Eastern type bread, tomatoes and black olives. Here I very much feel my way through what I thought it could combine with, and the result is quite astounding. I hope you enjoy this as much as we do. Serve with pita bread and crudités.

---

1 large clove garlic, roughly chopped
1 shallot, roughly chopped
1 cup ful medames beans - soak overnight, then boil until soft, drain & set aside
3 Tbsp (45 ml) cider vinegar
4 to 5 sun dried tomato halves
a dash of agave or maple syrup
1 Tbsp (15 m) ouzo (optional)
a pinch of salt (taste as you go along)
1 Tbsp (15 ml) olive oil
a pinch of chilli powder
a handful of chopped parsley

Place the shallot and garlic in your food processor, and process until you have small pieces. Then add the beans, and one ingredient at a time as you process the mixture. You should be left with a thick paste.
Spoon into a serving bowl, and refrigerate for several hours before serving. Enjoy !

SERVES 4

Spicy Hummus

This is an exciting and hot variation on my own hummus recipe, with a spicy twist to it. Hummus is a popular staple throughout the Middle East and North Africa, so I absolutely had to include it in this book also. I have been to so many restaurants that claim to be 'Middle Eastern' in some shape or form, and sorry to say, I have yet to be served a hummus that's worthy of its name.

---

2 cloves fresh garlic
14 oz (400 g) tin of chickpeas (washed and drained)
1½ Tbsp raw tahini (sesame paste)
juice of 1 fresh lemon
3 - 4 Tbsp (45 – 60 mL) extra virgin olive oil
salt to taste (this is a key ingredient – so don't omit this unless you have to)
½ tsp hot chilli powder (adjust according to how hot you like it
¼ tsp cumin powder
paprika powder, for garnishing/ dusting
4 Tbsp (60 mL) water - or more, depending on the consistency you prefer

Place the garlic in your food processor and process until very finely chopped. Then add the chickpeas, and continue to process until well broken down – you may need to scrape them down from the sides of your processor a few times.

Now add the tahini, and process further. Then add the salt, chilli powder, cumin powder, the lemon and oil, and the water bit by bit, until a thick paste is formed.

If you wish to have a thinner consistency, add more water, a little at a time, until you are happy with the texture - it ought to be smooth, and a little runny, in my opinion. Decant into a small serving bowl, place a black olive in the middle, and drizzle with olive oil. Refrigerate before serving.

SERVES 4

Fig Feast Salad with Ouzo, Orange & Lime Dressing

Salad

1 red onion, finely chopped

1 medium sized cooked beetroot, cut into small squares

a handful of fresh coriander/ cilantro, chopped

8-10 black fleshy Kalamatta olives, chopped

1 cup cucumber (with skin), chopped into squares

3 fresh figs, cut into wedges

½ an avocado, cut into small pieces

1 fresh red chilli, cut lengthways then chopped into small pieces

extra chopped coriander/cilantro, for garnishing

1/8 cup toasted pine nuts, for garnishing

the zest of 1 lemon, for garnishing

Dressing

the juice of a lime

the juice of an orange

4 Tbsp (60 ml) of Ouzo, or Pernod

2 Tbsp dark brown sugar (I used muscovado)

4 Tbsp (60 ml) extra virgin olive oil

a pinch or two of sea salt (to taste)

This is a magical salad with Middle Eastern tones, and a wonderful dynamic and sensual dressing. Although you may serve this as part of a main course, it's also delightful to have alongside my Spicy Hummus (see pg 33), and hot pita bread - the combination in itself will make an interesting and diverse main course. The trick with this salad is to ensure the figs are beautifully ripe, and taste the dressing before you pour it on the top, to make sure the salt and sweetness balance are just right. I love that the salad celebrates all tastes and textures together - a celebration of dynamic culinary sensuality - sweet, soft, bitter, crunchy, colourful, moist, chewy, creamy, aromatic and well, just perfect.

Salad

Once you have chopped all your salad ingredients and toasted your pine nuts, then just arrange them nicely in a medium sized salad bowl (except for the figs, which you can leave until the end), and toss very gently so that you don't over-crumble the avocado, and so that the beetroot does not 'over-bleed' onto the other ingredients. Then finally add the fig wedges, and grate the lemon zest in situ over your salad. Now throw the pine nuts on top, and make your dressing.

Dressing

Pour all the ingredients in a small saucepan, and whisk on a low heat - wait until it begins to caramelize, and then once it's done so, and is a little thick, allow to cool a little for 5 minutes. Then pour the magic dressing onto your salad. Serve and Enjoy !

SERVES 2 TO 3

Mouthwatering Middle Eastern-Style Salad

Edgy, zesty and mouthwatering to the full – this salad is perfect to eat as a main course, perhaps with a hot, crunchy wholemeal baguette – or as an accompaniment to virtually any meal you wish. Soaked in a rich and tasty dressing, I wanted to hit the palette on all its dimensions - sweetness, a tad of Middle Eastern spice, Mediterranean, and with lots of zang !!!

---

2 x 14 oz (400 g) tins of cannellini beans, drained and rinsed
12 cherry tomatoes, chopped
1 small red bell pepper, chopped
1 medium cucumber (washed, but not peeled), chopped into small pieces
2 spring onions, chopped
3 large cloves garlic, finely chopped
¾ cups of rucola (rocket), or radicchio lettuce
a handful of bean sprouts (optional)
the zest of 1 lemon, or other citrus fruit
8 basil leaves, chopped
a handful of fresh flat leaf parsley, finely chopped

NOTE : The trick with this salad is to cut each ingredient into very small squares/pieces.

Place all the salad ingredients in a bowl, then drench the salad with this dressing :

1 tsp dried mint
1 tsp curry powder
salt to taste (it will need it)
freshly ground pepper
1 Tbsp (15 mL) agave nectar
the juice of 2 lemons
extra virgin olive oil

Toss well, then transfer into a serving dish, and enjoy the sublime juices and flavours.

SERVES 4

Middle Eastern Tahini Salad

This wonderful salad goes well with just about every Middle Eastern dish. It's rich in flavour, very appetizing, and is one of my favourites. To spice it up, you can also add chopped hot pepper. You can serve this along side any veggie burger, or with falafel, accompanied by hot pita bread. It's a great one to serve up for guests, and also fantastic as an accompaniment to vegan BBQs.

---

2 tomatoes, cut into small or medium cubes
2 cucumbers, cut into small or medium cubes
2 cloves garlic, finely chopped
1 hot chili pepper, chopped
sea salt
½ cup (130 ml) tahini
the juice of 1 lemon
½ cup (125 ml) water
1 Tbsp dried mint
olive oil, to garnish

Dice up tomatoes and cucumbers, and combine them together in a medium bowl.

Crush your garlic, hot pepper and salt in a mortar. Add them in the bowl to your tomato and cucumbers. Meanwhile, make the tahini sauce.

Add the tahini, salt, lemon and water in a separate bowl and mix well.

This dressing takes a bit of stirring to blend well and become creamy. Pour dressing onto the salad, mix, and add the mint.

Place in the refrigerator for at least 20 minutes to allow the flavours to blend, and for the dressing to marinate with the tomatoes and cucumber. Serve with a swirl of olive oil on top. And Enjoy!

SERVES 4

My Fabulous Tabbouleh (Tabbouli)

I make my own version of Tabbouleh, and I love it. It's fresh, versatile and one handsome salad. Loved and enjoyed by millions of people worldwide, tabbouleh is a wonderful treat any time of the year - serve with hot pitta bread and My Spicy Hummus (see pg 33) or better still my Rich Spicy Bean Dip (see recipe pg 29). Enjoy !

---

1 cup bulgur wheat
boiling water (enough to cover the bulgur wheat in a bowl)
10 cherry tomatoes, quartered with a sharp knife
1 large bunch of parsley, very finely chopped
2 Tbsp fresh coriander/ cilantro, very finely chopped (optional)
1 cup cucumber, finely diced
2 spring onions (scallions) or red onions, finely chopped
1 red bell pepper, seeded and finely chopped
3 to 4 mint leaves, finely chopped - or around 1 tsp dried mint
juice of 1 lemon
1½ tsp fine sea salt
just under ½ cup (120 ml) olive oil
½ tsp maple syrup

Place your bulgur wheat in a bowl, then pour over enough boiling water to cover it. Allow it soak for around 15 minutes - it will absorb most of the water (if any is left, just drain the rest). Then place in a salad serving bowl of your choice, and allow it to cool for 10 minutes or so.

Now add the remaining ingredients, except for the olive oil, salt, lemon juice and maple syrup. Place these in a jar (jam jar size), close the lid tightly, and shake until blended. Then pour onto the salad and stir. Refrigerate and serve.

SERVES 4

Pasta Salad Me Feta

I love my feta cheese, and I love pasta - sometimes in the summer one fancies a carb rich, tasty pasta salad. But this is no ordinary pasta salad, and you will love it. It's easy to make, and a portion yields a meal in itself. Packed with richness of colour and flavour, this will be a spring and summer favourite in your home. Try and enjoy !

300g precooked pasta shells, drained and set aside
3 to 4 Tbsp (45-60 ml) extra virgin olive oil
1 Romano red pepper, cut lengthways
3 Tbsp tomato puree/paste
½ tsp curry powder
½ tsp chilli powder
¼ tsp ground cumin
sea salt to taste
1 Tbsp (15 ml) agave or maple syrup
10 Greek kalamata olives (or other similar fleshy olives), chopped
1 small red onion, finely chopped
1 spring onion, chopped
1 to 2 Tbsp vegan mayonnaise
1/8 cup raisins or sultanas
freshly chopped coriander/cilantro for garnishing
Isot Kurdish black pepper (optional) or crushed black pepper
¼ cup vegan feta cheese (around 125g), see my recipe on pg 67.

NOTE : If you wish to save time, instead making my feta, you can use tofu marinated overnight in olive oil, lemon and dill - just cut into squares. However, the result cannot compare to my own feta recipe.

First, precook your pasta, rinse, drain, and set aside.

Then heat your olive oil up in a large saucepan on a medium heat, then fry your red pepper.

Next, add the tomato puree/paste and your spices, mixing all the time. After a couple of minutes, add the pasta shells and lower the heat. After a further few minutes, turn off the heat, and allow your dish to cool down for 15 minutes.

Add the remaining ingredients, except for the feta, and mix well but gently. Now crumble on my feta cheese or tofu. Garnish, Serve & Enjoy !

SERVES 4

Tagine Superfood Salad

So, this is not a tagine, but it looked like it in situ, especially with the olives on the top, and that is where the name was born from. The chickpeas and stewed apricots made their way into this beautiful salad, and a combination of wonderful flavours came together to create a feast for the eyes, and a beautiful salad to serve when the table needs some cheer.

---

1 cup stewed apricots (each one cut into quarters prior to stewing)
1 large courgette/zucchini, chopped, fried, and set aside
1 red bell pepper, finely chopped, fried, and set aside
1 onion, thinly sliced
2 Tbsp tomato pureepaste
1 cup tinned (precooked) chickpeas
½ tsp garlic granules
1/8 tsp chilli powder
2 cups pre-cooked basmati rice (this dish also works well with couscous or bulgur wheat)
½ cup precooked red quinoa
½ avocado, chopped (optional)
4 Tbsp (60 ml) olive oil
1 Tbsp (15 ml) maple syrup
salt to taste
nuts of your choice - I suggest either toasted pine nuts or peanuts
olives, for decoration

Start by boiling or steaming your rice, and stewing your apricots in advance of cooking this dish.

Then heat your olive oil, fry the courgette and pepper, and set aside.

Now fry your onion until it softens, add the tomato puree/paste, and stir well. Add in the chickpeas, garlic granules and chilli powder, continuing to stir whilst you do so. Add the remaining ingredients, except for the apricots, and give it a good mix - a fork will do the job.

I suggest a wide-based serving bowl for this dish. Place your apricots in the bottom of the bowl, and build up the salad on top of the apricots into a pyramid mountain shape, then popping the olive on top. Serve hot or cold.

SERVES 4

Avgolemono – 'Egg' & Lemon Soup

This soup was made by my mother, and sometimes my father (a Greek Cypriot), using a whole chicken for the amazing stock it yielded. But those days are long gone, as being vegan means there is no need to take the life of any animal in order to satisfy your appetite. It was a favourite, and I wouldn't have been contented unless I could replicate it, and achieve a similar result. My mother made this when we were unwell. The alkalizing effect of the lemons, with their healing properties, were like a little miracle shot, always welcome and always full of the promise of recovery and wellness. I have made a few versions of it – and here's the best one. You can add some plain rice (around half a cup, add it in the soup water when boiling the veggies). I also add fake chicken pieces from time to time, for authenticity's sake - both the rice and fake chicken really make a hearty meal of this soup, but neither is obligatory.

---

a little extra virgin olive oil
2 medium sized courgettes/ zucchini, peeled and roughly chopped
1 small leek, roughly chopped
4 tsp vegetable stock
1½ ltr water
1 cup (250g) firm silken tofu, or ¾ cup of presoaked cashew nuts (drain and set aside)
the juice of a large lemon or of 2 medium sized lemons
salt to taste (don't omit)
a handful of fresh coriander/ cilantro
ground cinnamon, to dust on when serving

Fry your leek and courgettes on a low setting for 10 minutes until slightly softened.

Next, add the stock and water, and allow to boil gently until the veggies are soft. After a few minutes you can add in the chicken pieces and/or rice if you're using them. Once the veggies are ready, allow half an hour for everything to cool off.

Now transfer to a blender, adding in the remaining ingredients, except for the coriander and cinnamon, and process until rich and creamy. Now add in the coriander and pulse a few times - it needs to break down into very small pieces, but must not be totally processed otherwise the soup will turn green.

Heat up gently, serve into bowls, and dust with a little cinnamon. I recommend some crusty warm bread with this, and indulge . . .

NOTE : Or you can turn this recipe into the infamous Youvarlakia - Traditional Greek 'Meatball' Soup. Just make my keftedes (see recipe pg. 133), add ½ cup of pre-cooked white short grain rice to the keftedes mix, and fry them gently. When they cool, add around 3 balls per person to the soup. 1½ ladles of the soup in a soup bowl, with 3 balls in the middle of the plate - all served hot – a heartwarming winter treat !

SERVES 4

Sour Bulgur Trahana

Finally, a great vegan Greek Cypriot Trahana. My dad used to bring us some when he visited. The trahana itself is a wheat-based dried food usually made either with bulgur wheat or semolina and yoghurt, and then left to dry out completely. It is then used to form the basis of a delicious soup, made with stock, lemon juice, and sometimes pieces of Greek cheese (you could use my Lime Feta - see pg 67). My mother would make a super soup with my father's trahana, and we loved it. Here is my vegan version, which accompanies my Trahana Soup recipe below.

1¾ cups coarse bulgur wheat
1½ cups (375 ml) homemade vegan Greek yoghurt (see recipe pg 65)
1 cup (250 ml) soya milk
3 Tbsp fresh lemon juice
salt and freshly ground black pepper to taste
1/8 tsp asafoetida

Place all these ingredients in a saucepan, and stir on a low heat for 15 minutes or so until it resembles a thick porridge.

Preheat your oven to 250°F (120°C).

Meanwhile, prepare a tray, approximately 15 by 12 inches, by lining it with greaseproof paper (parchment), and spreading the mixture evenly over the base – it should be around a quarter of an inch in thickness.

Now place in your preheated oven bake for 2 to 3 hours, until your trahana is completely dry, with a brittle texture. However, if the edges begin to brown, break these off, and return your trahana to the oven until it is dry throughout.

Allow to cool down, then break into random pieces or chunks, and store in a clean, sterilized jar.

Refrigerate, and use when making trahana soup - it will keep in the fridge for several weeks if stored well.

SERVES 4

Trahana Soup

This is the soup to accompany my Trahana (see recipe above pg 49). Having had this often as a child, it is so personally rewarding for me to have successfully veganized it, and to be watching my own daughter gulping it down fills me with immense pleasure. It really is a special treat, especially during the winter months. You may also serve this with pieces of my pre-fried Vegan Haloumi (see recipe pg 69) for a more traditional Greek Cypriot treat.

---

1 cup of trahana (see recipe pg 49)
1½ ltr (2.65 pints) vegetable stock
1 cup homemade vegan Greek yogurt (see recipe pg 65) - allow the yogurt to become quite sour for this soup
salt to taste
the juice of 1 lemon

Place the stock, together with the trahana, in a casserole and heat them up gently. When the trahana has softened, take off the heat and place in your food processor, together with the rest of the ingredients. Add more yogurt for a richer taste, and adjust salt accordingly.
Serve hot with crunchy bread, or enjoy as is.

NOTE : The key to a good trahana soup is to ensure the yoghurt has gone sour. You may also wish to enhance this by adding a spoon or so of sauerkraut.

MAKES AROUND 20 BALLS OR 4 PORTIONS

Fiery Falafel

There are so many variations of falafel, and although it is thought to have originated in Egypt, it is now also a national dish in Palestine and Israel, and is popular throughout the Middle East. This recipe really captures the true essence of falafel, and is a staple for us – packed with protein, and with delicious spicy undertones. The falafel also freeze wonderfully – just be sure to first place them in the freezer on a pre-greased baking tray for a couple of hours, leaving space between each ball, before storing them in a freezer bag.

---

1 x 250g (9oz) pack dried chickpeas, pre-soaked overnight in water
2 cloves garlic
1 small onion, chopped
1 Tbsp fresh coriander/cilantro
1 Tbsp fresh parsley
2 tsp ground cumin
1 tsp salt
1 tsp molasses sugar
¼ tsp asafoetida powder
¼ tsp chilli powder
1 tsp fresh mint (or dried)
1 tsp ground coriander
¾ tsp bicarbonate of soda
3 to 4 handfuls of finely chopped breadcrumbs
corn oil, for frying

Soak your chickpeas in water the day before you make this recipe.

Now, I have found it best to process the ingredients in two sittings. First, process the chickpeas in your food processor until completely broken down. Then remove into a bowl and set aside.

Next, process the garlic and onion until finely chopped, then add all the remaining ingredients (except the corn oil, of course), and process until thoroughly combined.

Finally, add back in the chickpeas, and process until smooth.

Heat enough oil in a deep saucepan to deep-fry the falafel (be sure your oil is hot enough by testing one ball first), and fry the balls until golden on the outside. They should remain soft on the inside.

I serve mine with my own Fabulous Tabbouleh (see pg 41) and my Spicy Hummus (see pg 33) – and boy, do we have a feast !

SERVES AROUND 4

Lemon Drowned Roasted Potatoes

You will be staggered at the result of this simple dish. Can you imagine golden roast potatoes that burst with lemon in your mouth ? I'll say no more, other than this dish is happy partnered with any other savoury choice from this book..

---

5 medium sized potatoes, peeled, washed and drained
2 red onions, roughly chopped
the juice of 2 lemons
1 cup (250 ml) extra virgin olive oil
1 tsp hot mustard
a small clove garlic, finely chopped
½ tsp sea salt
fresh rosemary sprigs

First preheat your oven to 355ºF (180ºC).

Prepare the potatoes and onions as above. Then blend the lemon juice, olive oil, and mustard in your blender, until they turn whitish in colour. Arrange your potatoes, onions and garlic in a Pyrex oven dish (or similar), and pour on the lemon and olive oil mixture. Add salt to taste.

Garnish with rosemary, and bake until golden in your preheated oven. Enjoy !

SERVES 4

Roast Potatoes Smothered in Hot Chilli, Sundried Tomato & Zesty Garlic Sauce

It's possibly not the everyday line of thinking to consider potatoes a main course, and although this is an accompaniment, the rich sauce lends itself to making it filling and appetizing. So, all you then need to make this a main course is some hot pita bread, a drizzle of olive oil, some black olives and a green salad to crunch on. The flavours and texture, plus the aroma, will blow you away, and you will definitely come back for more !

---

5 spring onions (scallions), chopped
5 to 6 medium sized potatoes, peeled, washed and cut into wedges
3 cloves garlic, cut into slithers

For the Sauce
1 cup (250 ml) extra virgin olive oil
1 cup (250 ml) water
10 sun dried tomato halves
½ tsp ground chilli
½ tsp za'atar, or ground cumin
¼ tsp ground coriander
½ tsp fennel seeds
a drizzle of agave syrup, or equivalent
the juice of half a lemon
a pinch of sea salt (add more if you need to)

Garnish for the Top
the zest of half an orange (I cut mine into thinnish slithers)
isot pepper, or crushed black pepper, for sprinkling on top

First, preheat your oven to 250°F (120°C).

Then process the sauce ingredients in your food processor until smooth. You will need a suitable ovenproof dish – mine was a square Pyrex, 11 inches square by 2 inches deep.

First, evenly distribute the chopped spring onions across the base, and then arrange your potato wedges above the onions, followed by the garlic.

Pour the sauce mix on top, and with clean hands, massage the sauce into the potato wedges so that they are all completely smothered in the sauce. Now add the orange zest, drizzle some more olive oil, and garnish with pepper.

Place in your oven for a couple of hours, or until the potatoes are soft when you poke a fork in them.

Then turn your oven up to 400°F (200°C), until your potatoes are golden - around 20 minutes. Serve Hot, and Enjoy !

SERVES 3 TO 4

Scorched, Spiced & Caramelized Baby Tomatoes & Green Peppers

This is an awesome and simple to make dish - simply eat with your favourite bread, or for a gluten free meal, accompany with rice and quinoa. The juice is mesmerizing, and, dare I say it, it might be the only occasion that you lick your fingers, or even your plate clean. This can be served as a side plate or as a main dish, depending on appetite size or occasion – and it always works well alongside my Thick Vegan Greek Yoghurt (see recipe pg 65).

---

6 Tbsp (90 ml) extra virgin olive oil
6 medium sized green peppers, cut lengthways
1½ cups cherry tomatoes of your choice
¼ tsp garlic granules
¼ tsp ground cumin
¼ - ½ tsp sea salt
3 tsp dark sugar (I used muscovado)
2 Tbsp (30 ml) balsamic vinegar
a pinch of za'atar
fresh coriander/cilantro, for garnishing
sesame bark, for garnishing

Heat up the oil in a pan and fry the peppers until scorched. Add the tomatoes and the remaining ingredients, gently tossing the pan around, trying to avoid breaking the tomatoes. Allow the tomatoes to scorch a little too. The entire process will take approximately 20 minutes.

Garnish with fresh parsley or cilantro and some sesame bark. Now indulge yourself.

SERVES 4

Tender Baby Zucchini Smeared in Rose Harissa, Lime & Tomato

I bought the most amazing baby zucchinis (courgettes), firm and proud, and beautiful. So, I made a kind of stew out of them with flavours from the Middle East, and a twist of lime. Exotic food for the exotic palette. This dish just happened, and I am so happy with the result, so much so, I'm making this again soon. Well, the requests at the table have been firm and adamant, so I shall have to oblige ! Serve with warm pita bread sticks, and/or rice. Have a hummus on the go with this to, you know, dip here and there.

---

2 Tbsp (30 ml) extra virgin olive oil
2 to 3 medium sized shallots, cut lengthways
around 16 baby zucchinis/ courgettes
3 cloves garlic, cut fine, lengthways
½ tsp cumin
a cinnamon stick (optional)
2 to 3 Tbsp tomato puree/paste
Himalayan salt, or sea salt to taste
½ tsp muscovado sugar
½ cup (125 mL) water
1 tsp rose harissa (if you can't find it, use ordinary harissa, and add 2 drops of rose extract)
the juice of ½ small lime
2 cups baby spinach leaves (or 1 cup pre-cooked frozen spinach)
nigella seeds, for garnishing
freshly chopped parsley, or coriander/cilantro, for garnishing

Heat up your oil in a saucepan, and fry your shallots, until transparent. Then add your zucchini and garlic, and stir gently on a medium heat. Now add the cumin, cinnamon stick, and tomato puree/paste, and stir for a few seconds until they've combined.

Add the remaining ingredients, except for the spinach and lime. When the baby zucchinis have begun to soften (after about 25 minutes), add the spinach and cover – and simmer for 15 minutes.

When the sauce has thickened, the dish is ready.

MMMmmmmm !

Sundried Tomatoes

Tomatoes were originally salted and dried to preserve the fruit, though we now enjoy the concentrated, intense flavour as a completely separate ingredient from the fresh tomato. And an added bonus is that the tomatoes in their dried form lose none of their nutritional value – and are high in lycopene, antioxidants, and vitamin C.

These are great to cook with, for example smeared on Italian ciabatta bread or similar Mediterranean breads, and can be used to pump up any sauce, or as a great topping for pasta. Or even simply stuff a hot pita bread with them, a drizzle of oil, and lashes of my Feta Cheese (see pg 67). This, together with some olives on the side, would make a great snack. Personally, for my sundried tomatoes, I prefer to use baby zengulis, as they are packed with flavour, and produce delicious bite-sized treats.

50-100 baby zenguli tomatoes, cut in half - they should be ripe, but firm (as many as you like - I did a batch of about 150 tomatoes)
1 to 2 cloves garlic, sliced (again, as much garlic as you like)
salt to taste
extra virgin olive oil

First, pre-heat your oven to 225ºF (100ºC).
Then cut the tomatoes in half, adding fresh garlic, olive oil, and salt to taste.
Prepare a shallow oven tray by lining it with greaseproof paper, then evenly distribute your tomatoes flat across the surface area, ensuring they don't overlap.
Pop them in the oven for an hour, then turn off the oven, and leave the tomatoes to sit overnight in the warmth of the oven.
Remove from oven, decant into a large Tupperware container, and place in the fridge, where they'll last for months.

MAKES 1 LITRE (35 FL OZ)

Thick Vegan Greek Yoghurt

Yoghurt is a staple for so many, that the quest to find a good substitute when I became vegan some years ago briefly became an obsession. I worked my way through the commercially produced offerings, which at the time didn't even come close to the mark (the situation has improved more recently). Nut-based dairy alternatives have been around for many years, though primarily as cheeses and milks, but nut-based yoghurt looked a bit more of a challenge. However, I have found this simple recipe to consistently give the best results. I used to make my yoghurt with almonds, until I once ran out, and made it with cashews, and it yielded the most rich, thick and creamy taste and consistency. I haven't looked back since. I have also experimented with various non-dairy milks, and was using coconut for a while, but find the soya the better option for us, only because it gets the family vote. So I would stick to either almond, coconut or soya milk, to be safe.

I do use my Vitamix high-speed blender (you will need a blender powerful enough to completely pulverize the nuts), and I also invested in a yoghurt maker with a nice large bowl, as I couldn't be doing with fiddling around anymore with the small containers that come with most yoghurt makers. I would also recoomend a digital food thermometer.

120g (4½ oz) cashew nuts, washed and drained – alternatively you can use 90g (3¼ oz) cashews, and 30g (1 oz) almonds. If you're using almond milk, increase the nut total quantity to 150g (112g cashews, 38g almonds, if you're mixing the nuts)
700ml (23.5 fl oz) non-dairy milk (I prefer to use Alpro soya unsweetened, though coconut or almond milks work just as well – particularly if you can't take soya)
150g (5.5oz) non-dairy plain yoghurt

Very simple. Place your washed and drained cashews (and almonds if you're using them) in your high speed blender, along with around a third of the non-dairy milk. Pulverize on full speed for a few minutes, until you can see the nuts have broken down. Then add in the remaining milk, and continue to blend on full speed for a few more minutes, ensuring there are no nut pieces remaining.

Transfer to a medium saucepan, and heat the mixture on a low to medium heat, stirring all the time with a hand milk whisk. You will also need to read the temperature using your digital thermometer, and when it reaches 110°F (43°C), take your pan off the heat. Then stir in your yoghurt, ensuring that you mix it well.

Decant into your yoghurt jars or bowl, and follow the directions with your machine for how long to leave it on. My yoghurt takes around 4½ to 5 hours to become rich and creamy. You may find it separates, with the 'water' at the bottom. If so, give it a good mix, let it cool down, and store in the fridge, where it lasts for anything up to a week.

Always remember to leave enough yoghurt from your existing batch to start the next – the important thing is that all your equipment and containers are meticulously clean, and that you have a live bacteria to start each batch you make. It's great fun as an ongoing pastime, and I've never enjoyed yoghurt as much as I do now !

Lime Infused Feta Cheese

Feta cheese is a staple in Greece, and accounts for about 70% of the Greeks' cheese consumption. Its salty, tangy taste, and dry, crumbly texture, make it ideal to cut into a Greek salad, or include as an ingredient in dishes such as Spanakopita – I've included it in my version in this book (see pg. 121), and also in several other of my main course dishes. I've added lime juice into this one, which just takes it to another magical dimension !

120g raw cashews (presoak for a few hours)
115g almonds (presoak for a few hours)
¼ cup (60 ml) refined coconut oil – important to use a pure, refined coconut oil as this will have no taste *
2 vegan probiotic pills – such as L-acidophilus
½ cup (120 ml) very warm water
20g nutritional yeast
1 Tbsp 15 ml) extra virgin olive oil
1 tsp (15g) Himalayan salt
juice of ½ lime
a few drops of agave syrup
chilli seeds or nigella seeds
drizzle of olive oil at end

Marinade
extra virgin oil mixed with herbs of your choice, a slither of garlic, and to give it some edge, freshly squeezed lime.

* Please look for a fair trade, cruelty-free brand of coconut oil

Place the nuts in a powerful blender with the water and process until smooth. To achieve a good, smooth consistency, you'll need to scrape down the edges to keep the mixture moving, and process to the point where it's silky smooth, adding the rest of the ingredients as you go along.

Taste – and if you're happy, all you have to do now is spoon your mixture into a muslin cloth – and allow to drain over a basin, or bowl, for around 12 hours.

Then remove the muslin cloth, place your cheese in a lightly greased dish, and air dry in your oven at 210ºF (100ºC) for half an hour. Keep an eye on it to be sure that it doesn't turn golden - the reason for baking it is so that it forms an outer rind, plus when it cools, it'll cut better when serving.

Once cool - refrigerate for several hours before serving.

NOTE : This feta cheese will last for a few weeks in the fridge, so long as it's stored in olive oil in an airtight container.

Vegan Haloumi

Haloumi originated from Cyprus, but is today popular throughout Greece, Turkey and the Eastern Mediterranean. It is traditionally made from a mixture of goats' and sheeps' milks, though more recently made from cows' milk, due to its more ready availability. It is a semi-hard cheese, which is often fried or grilled in slices, as it has a very high melting point.

Given my own Cypriot roots, it has been a personal challenge for me to create a vegan version of haloumi that I feel is worthy of its name. I hope I have managed to achieve this with this recipe, which all my family love (a definite feather in my cap, I can assure you). Hope you enjoy it also - I suggest serving with a fresh and crunchy green salad, extra virgin olive oil, and of course a generous squeeze of fresh lemon juice.

---

2 cups of stale white bread (not crusts), processed until fine crumbs
1 Tbsp nutritional yeast
4 Tbsp vegan yoghurt (see recipe pg 65)
2 Tbsp (30 ml) refined coconut oil *
1 Tsp salt
½ pack (175g) firm silken tofu
1 cup (250 mL) warm water
½ tsp citric acid
3½ Tbsp agar powder
fresh lemon juice
extra virgin olive oil

* Please look for a fair trade, cruelty-free brand of coconut oil

You will need a suitable ovenproof dish to bake the cheese in – mine was a small rectangular one measuring approximately 7 x 5 x 1½ inches. You will then need a second dish large enough for the first dish to comfortably fit inside, which you will then half fill with hot water, in order to cook the cheese bain-marie.

I suggest pre-oiling your cheese dish, lining it with greaseproof paper, and even oiling the inner face of the paper, to be sure you have no problems with sticking.

Now preheat your oven to 300°F (150°C), then process the bread and nutritional yeast in your food processor until almost a powder. Add in the remaining ingredients, blend further, and decant into your oiled container. Then place this into your larger dish half filled with hot water, and carefully place in the middle of your oven. Bake for 25 to 30 minutes with foil on top, then uncover, lower the temperature to 210°F (100°C), and leave in oven for further 15-20 minutes. Remove from oven - your haloumi is ready when it's solid on top but still spongy, but be sure not to let it brown.

Allow to completely cool, cover with fresh piece of foil, and leave overnight in the fridge.
To serve, slice into roughly ½ inch slices, and fry gently on both sides until golden in a non-stick pan.

SERVES 4

Vegan Tzatziki

It is likely that tzatziki originates from Ancient Greece - we know that ancient Atheneans made yoghurt (as easily as they made cheese) and mixed it with spices and garlic or onion. However, the origin of this simple dip, along with many other traditional recipes (for example, dolma, yaprak, lukum, yoghurt, baklava, etc.) is a contentious issue, as there are Turkish equivalents of many of these – yogun, Baklagu, dolama, etc., 'cacik' being the Turkish version of tzatziki.

Anyhow, regardless of its origins and etymology, this is my vegan version of a delicious, simple dip that can accompany almost any Greek or Middle Eastern dish – and because of its neutral, gentle taste, it can also serve to take the fire out of the more spicy mains, in the same way that raita does in Indian cuisine.

½ cucumber, finely diced
375g (13 oz) plain vegan yogurt (see recipe pg 65)
1 clove garlic, very finely chopped
1 Tbsp fresh mint, chopped (freshly chopped dill can also be used as well as, or instead of)
2 Tbsp (30 ml) extra virgin olive oil
salt to taste

Finely chop your cucumber, and add with your finely chopped garlic into a medium-sized mixing bowl, along with your other ingredients. Stir well, and transfer into your serving bowl, before refrigerating covered overnight.

Simple Vegan Grated Cheese

If you're unable to find a vegan grated cheese, you can use :

1 cup raw cashews
½ cup nutritional yeast
1 tsp sea salt
½ tsp garlic granules or powder

Place the ingredients in your food processor, and process until it resembles grated cheese. Store in an airtight container in the fridge, where it will last for up to 2 weeks.

OPINE
INOX

Pastourma (Pastirma) with Ouzo

My dad always enjoyed his meat, and whenever we hadn't seen him for a lengthy period, he'd often come with a bag of goodies. Pastourma was one such delight, and it lasted for ages as my mother cut away slice after slice. This is my plant-based alternative - full of the same delightful mouthfeel and flavour of the original. My pastourma will last for many days in the fridge, and is great served with Greek salad, as a sandwich filler, or with figs and melon. Great also in pita bread with my Feta Cheese (see pg 67). In Egypt it is served as a topping on pizza - I've tried it that way and it rocks. I have even served it as part of a pasta sauce. This recipe is worth the time for the reward it gives back.

---

9 soya fettine (small fillets), or 3 cups of flavour-free dehydrated soya chunks, soaked overnight, then wrung out thoroughly
3 vegan sausages (if these are not available use 4 slices of bread instead)
marinated in :
¾ cup (188 ml) refined coconut oil *
3 tsp minced fresh garlic
¼ tsp garlic granules (yes, that's more garlic)
1½ tsp salt (may sound a lot, but it is needed)
1 tsp smoked paprika
2 tsp (10 ml) maple syrup
2 tsp fenugreek
1 tsp cumin powder
½ tsp all spice
1 tsp coriander seeds
1 heaped Tbsp beetroot powder
½ tsp guar gum
1 Tbsp (15 ml) ouzo

Rub Ingredients
2 tsp beetroot powder
1½ tsp garlic powder or fine granules
1½ tsp salt
½ tsp icing/confectioner's sugar
1 tsp ground smoked paprika

* Please look for a fair trade, cruelty-free brand of coconut oil

Blend the marinade well. Then cut the sausages into slices, and the fettine, if using, into smallish pieces. Fully immerse these in the marinade in a glass dish, and cover. If using soya chunks, simply immerse them in the marinade with the sausage slices, as there is no need to cut these smaller. Then allow your faux meat to marinate for a couple of hours in the fridge (overnight if you wish).
Remove from fridge, and preheat your oven to 300°F (150°C).
Now process the chilled fettine (or soya chunks) and sausages in your food processor until they've broken down. Then add half of the marinade, and process for around 20 seconds. Place the rest of the marinade in a small bowl and cover. Remove mixture from the processor into a large bowl, and refrigerate for half an hour, so it can set better. Form into the shape of a pastourma, as in my picture, and place in a small rectangular dish (mine was around 7 x 5 x 1½ inches deep), lined with greaseproof paper, and use a spatula to flatten it. Or wrap the mixture in greaseproof paper (parchment paper) and scrunch the edges, and shape into a large semi-circle, i.e. the bottom end of the sausage will be flat against the dish.
Bake in your preheated oven for 40 minutes. Then remove from oven, allow your sausage to cool for at least one hour, then place in foil and refrigerate overnight. Then the next day unwrap, and rub with the rub mix. Take out of fridge and place in your freezer for half an hour. Then uncover, and rub the remaining oil all around the pastourma, and let it sit for a few minutes in the fridge.
Then rub in a mixture of the herbs and spices - allow it to cool uncovered in the fridge for a day or two until a kind of rind is formed.
You will need to wait overnight before you can slice and serve this. It will not be as dense as the non-vegan version, but it should slice nevertheless.

MAKES 4 SAUSAGES

Loukaniko Greek Sausage

This is my own take on this traditional Greek sausage – though like any country sausage, there are many possible variations, depending on the region and the individual cook. It is often flavoured with orange peel, fennel seed, and various other dried herbs and seeds, and sometimes smoked over aromatic woods, and served as a mezze, sliced and fried.

½ cup short grain white rice
3 cloves garlic
6 slices of stale white bread
1 Tbsp smoked paprika
1 tsp asafoetida (optional)
½ tsp salt
1 tsp chilli powder
a sprinkle of aniseed
1 tsp garlic granules
1 tsp coriander seeds
2 Tbsp kappa carrageenan
¼ tsp guar gum
2 Tbsp wheat gluten (you can find this from Amazon if not available locally)
12 sundried tomatoes
1 tsp (5 mL) coconut oil *
2 tsp (10 mL) agave syrup
2 Tbsp (30 mL) medium dried sherry
1 tsp (5 mL) teriyaki sauce
1 tsp (5 mL) liquid smoke
1 Tbsp grated fresh orange zest

* Please look for a fair trade, cruelty-free brand of coconut oil

First, prepare your rice – boiled to al dente, then drain and set aside to cool.

Now process the garlic in your food processor, then the same with the bread until crumbs are formed. Remove into a large bowl.
Next, add the dried ingredients to the bread in the bowl.

Place the sundried tomatoes in your processor, and process until broken down into a paste. Add in the coconut oil, and process until smooth. Then add the rest of the wet ingredients and process.
Now add the sundried tomato mixture to the bread mixture, and using clean hands, gently mix until blended.

Now form into 4 cylinders, cover with cling film, then do so again with the edges twisted. Repeat the same procedure with foil (making sure the edges are properly sealed) and steam for 2 hours.

Allow to cool completely – then place on a large plate, and refrigerate overnight uncovered, so that they dry out further in the fridge.
I then suggest either frying them in a non-stick pan with a teaspoon of olive oil – or thread them on to skewers (they will be malleable enough) with alternating ¾ inch slices of bell pepper, mushroom, onion, and zucchini, and then grill or barbeque them. Before serving, remove from skewers. They work well in pita bread, served with a Greek salad, and slices of my haloumi fried (see pg 69), with lashes of fresh lemon juice.
Then place in a Tupperware or other similar airtight container, and store in the fridge for 7-10 days, or you can freeze them for up to 2 months.

NOTE : You could also add a little vermouth and/or anise. As these are vegan sausages, they will not be as firm as meat ones, but they work very well all the same.

Our Local Maltese Baker

We have been blessed for the past 17 years or so with possibly the best baker in Malta, around the corner from us. I should explain that Maltese bread (hobza tal- Malti) is something of an institution in Malta, and the bakers take great pride in their craft. Our one still bakes in a wood oven, and the bakery is a family business that has been running for generations.

Although not strictly Greek or Middle Eastern, I think Malta could just slip through the net with its strong Arabic influences, and the long line of Arabic rule, dating back to the Phoenicians between the 7th and 4th centuries BC, the Fatimids (Muslims from North Africa) for over 200 years from 870 to 1091, and the Tukish Ottoman Empire from the early 16th century right through to almost the beginning of the 19th century. The language betrays this heritage, with many words remaining the same as their Arabic equivalents.

Anyhow, the real relevance of showing you this marvelous bread, is that I have used loaves from this fabulous craftsman many times over to accompany my recipes, both in this book, my blog recipes, and also in 'Mouthwatering Vegan' – so I thought it only fit to introduce my friendly baker round the corner, Mario.

Maltese Hobz biz-zejt (literally translated 'Bread with Oil') - bread smeared with fresh tomato, drizzled with olive oil, and served with black olives, and chopped garlic & mint

MAINS

opposite page Stuffed Romano Peppers

SERVES 4

Chilli & Orange Zest Filletti in Rich White Wine & Aniseed Sauce

This is a semi-hot dish I created. Having soaked some soya filletti chunks in hot water for half an hour, I then wrung them out well, and sliced them lengthways with a sharp knife to create a kind of pull effect. I assembled some ingredients that I felt were complementary, yet created enough of a contrast to make the flavours sing well on the tongue. Slithers of fresh orange zest, dry white wine, aniseed and chilli. I added a wonderful mixture of porcini mushrooms to add dynamic to the texture too. The result - a rich sauce fit for marriage with spaghetti to soak up all the incredible delicate juices, or simple rustic Mediterranean bread. You can have this served on a bed of jasmine rice, or else with my Lemon Drowned Potatoes (see recipe pg. 55). What could be better ? A truly stunning dish.

---

extra virgin olive oil
1 medium sized red onion, chopped
4 to 5 cloves garlic, cut into slithers
1 cup of soya filletti (or similar faux meat strips), soaked, wrung out, and cut into thin slices
¼ tsp chilli powder
1/8 tsp ground aniseed
1/8 tsp all spice
2 to 4 whole dried red chillies, very finely chopped
½ tsp garlic granules (yes, more garlic)
2 Tbsp tomato puree/paste, dissolved in ½ cup (125 ml) hot water
1 cup porcini mushrooms (choose a mixture) - leave whole if very small, but cut if they're larger than an inch diameter
¾ cup (175 ml) dry white wine
Himalayan salt to taste
1 tsp stevia, or other sweetener of your choice
¼ cup either golden sultanas or whole raisins
1 tsp veg thickener (such as Bisto) dissolved in ½ cup (125 ml) water

Gently heat up the olive oil in a large saucepan, and add the onion. Stir until transparent, then add your garlic, and within a minute add the slithers of soya 'meat'.

Now add all the spices, the garlic granules, and a little more olive oil.

Next, stir in the tomato puree/paste mixture, and let the 'meat' absorb it. Add the wine, and the rest of the ingredients, except for the Bisto and water mixture.

Allow to simmer until it reduces, and then slowly stir in the Bisto mix about 15 minutes later. Again, simmer for a further 20 minutes on a low heat.

Taste for salt, and serve.

SERVES 4-6 SELF-CONTROLLED, ALTRUISTIC ADULTS

Baked Fasolia Pie with 'Feta' & Black Olives

The joy and culinary bliss that this recipe brings will have you going back for more at least twice - and that's even if you're on a diet - because this pie is quite simply the best. Packed with amazing flavours, rich earthy colours and textures, and a beautiful aroma that hits home the minute you cut through it. The base layer of potato is a bonus in this dish, and adds a wonderful creamy texture, which I find so delightful in savoury pies.

I confess to have used the Jus-Rol shortcrust pastry, because I love it. But by all means, make your own, or buy whichever brand you prefer, but check for sure it's vegan.

You will need a 9″ non-stick oven pie dish

around 4 medium sized potatoes, precooked
vegan margarine
salt to taste
extra virgin olive oil
1 medium red onion, finely chopped
1 small carrot, grated or cut into small pieces lengthways
1 stick of celery, chopped
500g (17.5 oz) shortcrust pastry
1 clove garlic, chopped, and I also used ½ tsp garlic granules
2 Tbsp rich tomato puree/paste
a pinch of dried dill (about 1/8 tsp)
a pinch of chilli powder
a pinch of dried aniseed (about 1/8 tsp)
1 cup (250ml) water
1 tin (240g net) cannellini beans - you may use other beans such as haricot
2 sticks of cinnamon
500g vegan shortcrust pastry
10 Kalamatta black olives (the salty ones) - roughly chopped
½ cup of my Lime Feta Cheese (see recipe pg. 67)

First, pre-boil your potatoes. When soft enough, cut into ¼ inch slices, and whilst hot, melt in some vegan margarine or some olive oil, and a little salt, and set these aside.
Now heat your oil in a large saucepan, and fry your onion until it turns slightly transparent. Then add your carrots and celery, stir in your tomato puree/ paste, mix for a few minutes, and add your herbs and spices. Next, add the remaining ingredients, except for your olives and feta cheese, pouring in your water a little at a time. Lower the heat, and simmer gently for 30 minutes. You should be left with a nice rich sauce at the end.
Next, using clean hands, crumble or slice the 'feta' into your sauce, then allow to cool for 10-15 minutes.
Meanwhile, preheat your oven to 355ºF (180ºC).
To prepare the pastry, first pre-grease your dish with a little vegetable oil. Then take your dough, and cut it in half, making sure that one of the halves is about 20 percent larger than the other, so you can use it to cover the base and sides of the pie. Roll it out, and place into the pre-greased dish. Then evenly distribute the potato slices over the pastry base, and pour your sauce on top of the potatoes.
Now roll out the remaining dough, and close the pie with it. Take a fork and pinch the edges all around the pie, and finally pinch some holes with the fork on the surface, to allow the pie to breathe.
Place in your preheated oven until it turns golden. Remove from oven, and allow to rest for 5-10 minutes before cutting and serving, whilst you plan how to deal with the stampede for seconds . . .

SERVES 4-6

Epic Sweet Potato Kibbeh with Cheese & Sundried Tomato

2 sweet potatoes, peeled, cut into squares, and steamed till soft
1 to 2 Tbsp vegan margarine
2 tsp salt (or as you wish, remember the potatoes are sweet)
½ tsp ground cumin
1½ cups bulgur wheat - place in a medium sized bowl and cover with hot water until the water is absorbed (for a gluten free option, use millet or quinoa - cook according to instructions on packet and then set aside in a bowl
2 cups grated vegan cheese of your choice (I used our own MIDAS Parmejano)
1 medium sized onion, grated or very finely chopped
1 Tbsp nutritional yeast
2 Tbsp flat leaf parsley, finely chopped
6 to 8 sun dried tomato halves, chopped
4 Tbsp unbleached plain flour, or for a gluten free version, use gluten free flour mix
¼ cup pistachio nuts, lightly broken, for garnishing
olive oil for drizzling

I have seen a number of kibbeh's the last few years in books and online - in the end my two sweet potatoes had to find a culinary home. So I made this wonderful Middle Eastern inspired dish - and I can say to you with all honesty, it's one of the most delicious dishes of its kind I have ever had ! Every mouthful is a celebration, and I am so pleased it worked so well, so much so, that I am going to share it with you now.
I served ours with my Fabulous Tabbouleh (see recipe pg 41).

Place the hot steamed potatoes in a large bowl with margarine and salt, and mash until smooth, then add the remaining ingredients and mix with a large spoon.

Preheat your oven to 400°F (200°C).

Then, using clean hands, give your mix a further mash.

Now grease an ovenproof dish and spoon in the mixture. Flatten the top and mark the edges with a fork, garnish with nuts, and drizzle on some olive oil. Score the portions gently (not deeply) with a sharp knife.

Place in your hot preheated oven for 45 minutes, or until golden.

Remove from oven, and allow to cool for 20 minutes at least, before cutting into portions and serving.

My Legendary 'No-Lamb' Middle Eastern-Style Bake

I was in a 'bake' super zone when I made this wondrous bake. I merged the flavours of the Middle East, in particular a touch of the Greek and Turkish - I simply couldn't believe the result, and I'm quite sure you're going to love it. Make, bake, and also share with non-vegans !

SERVES 4-6

2 Tbsp (30 ml) olive oil
3 spring onions, chopped
3 cloves garlic, chopped
¼ red bell pepper, chopped
2 Tbsp tomato puree/paste
1 400g tin tomato pulp
2½ cups vegan mince meat/ground crumbles (or use a mixture of crushed pecans and lentils)
6 to 8 sundried tomato halves, chopped
½ tsp smoked paprika
1 Tbsp coconut oil *
1 tsp dried mint
1 tsp cumin powder
¼ cup (60 ml) water
salt to taste

'Cheese Sauce'

2 cups (500 ml) soya milk, or other non-sweetened milk (I used Alpro)
1 Tbsp all purpose plain flour
3 Tbsp nutritional yeast
2 Tbsp (30 ml) olive oil
½ tsp fine garlic granules
salt (don't omit)
a knob of vegan butter/margarine
¼ tsp turmeric powder
1 tsp vegetable stock powder or granules (try Kallo)
a little water if needed

Vegetables

1 large aubergine/eggplant, cut lengthways
2 medium courgettes/zucchini, cut lengthways

Extras

olive oil for greasing
2 cups vegan grated cheese
paprika powder

* Please look for a fair trade, cruelty-free brand of coconut oil

---

Sauce

First, heat up the oil in your frying pan (I used a cast iron skillet), and fry your spring onions until slightly golden.
Next, stir in your garlic, and mix until it is slightly golden.
Then add your red pepper and tomato puree/paste, and mix for a couple of minutes. Now add your vegan mince/ground crumble, and mix again.
Then add the remaining ingredients, and simmer gently for 20 minutes until the sauce thickens. Taste for salt, and set aside.

Cheese Sauce

Place all the ingredients in a 'milk' pan and whisk.
Heat the mixture up, mixing virtually non-stop, until you have a thickish consistency. Lower the heat, and continue cooking for a further minute or so.

To Assemble

Pre-heat your oven to 375°F (190°C)
Grease a suitable Pyrex (or similar) oven dish (mine was around 7" diameter, 3" deep) then place the aubergine slices across the base and sides of the dish, so that they overlap one another. Then add half your 'meat' sauce to the base, followed by the courgette slices, and half of the cheese sauce (try to even the ingredients out with the back of a large spoon).
Next, add the rest of the 'meat' sauce, then cover with a mixture of the remaining aubergine and courgette slices - don't worry, there won't be enough to seal it, but that's exactly what we want for the top - a random mix of things.
Then add the remaining 'cheese' sauce, any grated or cut up vegan cheese, and finally sprinkle on some paprika with a drizzle of olive oil.
Bake in the oven for 30 to 40 minutes, and remove when it's really golden.
Allow to cool down for 20 minutes before serving, as it will be piping hot.
This can also be made a day ahead. Enjoy !

SERVES 4

My Iranian Style 'No Beef' Aubergine Stew (Koresh Bademjan)

I created a Middle Eastern style stew, but with different spices. We devoured it in one sitting, and loved it - it was inspired by my love for all things Middle Eastern, the stews I had at family sittings as a child, and my insatiable love for curry spices and East Indian food. It's fast to make, and you'll love this. It has a little trick to make the vegan meat meatier, and it worked well.

Serve on hot rice. I used short grain brown for us, boiled it and then fried it in a little olive oil, vegan butter, and some turmeric. I wanted to crunch it up a little, and it created a fabulous dynamic of flavours and textures.

---

1 cup soya chunks - I used dried 'fettine' (slices)
2 Tbsp (30ml) extra virgin olive oil
1 large white onion, finely chopped
6 cloves garlic, finely chopped
1 tsp coriander seeds
2 tsp curry powder
¼ tsp asafoteida (optional)
½ tsp cardamom seeds, crushed - or the ground type will do
½ tsp ground turmeric
¼ tsp Isot ground pepper - use chillies if you can't find this
2 Tbsp (30ml) dry white wine
1 very large aubergine/eggplant, peeled, cut into 1 inch squares
3 large Tbsp tomato puree/paste
1 tsp muscovado sugar, or maple syrup, or other sweetener
1½ cups petit pois
¾ cup (185 ml) water
the juice of ½ lime
a cinnamon stick (remove after cooking, if you wish)
sea salt to taste
the zest of ½ lime
fresh chopped coriander/cilantro, to garnish

First, rehydrate your dried 'meat', by soaking it in very hot water for 10-15 minutes (but follow the instructions any instructions on the packet for exact guidelines). Then drain the water, wring out excess water from your 'meat' chunks, and if you wish, cut them into smaller pieces, using a pair of sharp kitchen scissors.

Next, fry your onions, and when transparent, add the garlic and the spices. Now add the soya pieces/chunks, and let them pick up the spices for around 2-3 minutes, then pour in the wine, and allow them to cook for a further minute or so as you stir.

Begin to stir in the aubergine/eggplant squares, and continue to stir on and off for the next few minutes, until they start to soften. You can add the tomato puree/paste now, as well as the sugar, and a little more oil if needed, as the aubergine drinks much of it up, and stir in the peas whilst you're at it.

Now add your water, lime juice, and the remaining ingredients, and allow to simmer for half an hour or so. You should be left with a thick stew, and an amazing aroma.

Serve on hot rice, as outlined above. Bon Appétit !

SERVES 2

Vegan Shakshuka – 'Breakfast in Israel'

This recipe is a beautiful staple in Israel, very often eaten for breakfast, or as a light lunch. Its origins are thought to have been rooted in Africa – some say Tunisia, others Morocco – but, in any case, the Israelis love a good debate about recipes, and they certainly love their food, as do I. So, here is my vegan version – in fact, the first vegan shakshuka in the world (as far as I know, when I created it a couple of years ago), which has already become a staple in our household. It is dedicated to the many people in Israel who have embraced veganism, and to my very good friend Gary Yourofsky, who has helped to enlighten so many in that wonderful country to the benefits of veganism.
This dish takes a bit of preparation, but is worth the time and effort for the result.

¼ tsp cumin seeds, dry roasted
olive oil for frying
¼ tsp asafoetida
½ tsp smoked paprika
¼ tsp chilli powder
¼ tsp coriander seeds
1 large onion, peeled and thinly sliced
1 medium red pepper, thinly sliced (get long Romano ones if you can)
1 medium yellow pepper, thinly sliced
½ a chilli pepper
2 cloves garlic
2 tsp muscovado sugar
2 bayleaves
¼ tsp dried or fresh thyme
2 tsp flat leaf parsley, finely chopped (reserve some for garnishing)
2 tsp coriander/cilantro leaves, chopped
3 ripe tomatoes, finely chopped
¼ tsp saffron strands
1 Tbsp tomato puree/paste
sea salt to taste
a little water, if needed

NOTE : Prepare your 'egg yolk' and 'egg white' in advance, or whilst the shakshuka is simmering to thicken (see recipe on pg 93)

First, dry-roast your cumin seeds in a hot skillet pan, or cast-iron frying pan, until they start to emit their wonderful aroma.

Then add your oil, and fry your other spices - chilli peppers, asafoetida, smoked paprika, and coriander seeds, but not the saffron strands. Add your onion, and when it's become transparent, add the peppers and garlic, and stir until they're a bit scorched.

Next, stir in your muscovado sugar and herbs, continue to cook for a few minutes, before adding the remaining ingredients, and cooking for a further 15 minutes on a fairly high heat, stirring regularly. Then lower the heat, and allow the sauce to thicken nicely.

Check for seasoning - be sure that your sauce is a little sweet, but also hot and edgy, and that it has enough salt.

Then make an indent with a large spoon in the thickened sauce for your two ready prepared 'egg whites' (see recipe below). Gently place each 'egg white' in the indentations, spoon in the 'yolk' mixture, and season with pepper. Garnish with finely chopped parsley, serve and Enjoy !

MAKES 2 EGGS

Vegan 'Fried Eggs'

The first of its kind, I created this recipe several years ago. Works well as an accompaniment to many dishes, and truly takes the place for those who cannot eat eggs, for whatever reason.

Ingredients for the 'Yolk'

2 Tbsp vegan dried instant mashed potatoes, dehydrated flakes or powder
7 Tbsp (105 mL) hot water, though you may need a tiny bit more
1 tsp vegan margarine
½ tsp pea protein
1 tsp nutritional yeast
¼ tsp turmeric
¼ tsp kala namak salt, otherwise known as black salt – it has a sulphuric "egg" flavour, so it's essential for this recipe (you should find this at your local Indian or Asian grocery store)
¾ tsp egg replacer (Orgram in the UK or Australia, or Ener-G in the US)
1 tsp sunflower or canola oil (not olive oil, as that would alter the taste)

Ingredients for the 'White'

1 cup firm silken tofu (I use Mori-Nu non-GMO)
TIP : you may wish to place the packet of tofu in the freezer for 30 minutes prior to opening – it makes for a firmer cut
1 Tbsp plain unbleached flour
1 Tbsp (15 ml) vegan milk
a pinch of salt
extra oil for frying

The 'Yolk'

Make up your mashed potato mix with the water, add margarine and the other ingredients including the oil, and mash using a fork until consistency resembles hard-boiled egg yolk - but it should be thick in consistency (there is a reason for this). Then spoon out half of the mixture into a separate bowl, and set aside.

The 'White'

Process the above ingredients in your food processor, and then spoon into a hot pre-greased non-stick pan.

When firm on the base, flip and press down with a metal spatula, and when it's solid, remove.

Allow to cool, and cut out the centre using a small round cookie cutter (mine was 7cm)

SERVES 4-6

My Beautiful Baked Fattoush

I created a marriage of Fattoush, a Levantine bread salad usually made with mixed greens and other seasonal vegetables, converted into a bake with Greek overtones – with a Greek Feta cheese sauce. And behold, they instantly lived together in Middle Eastern harmony. The flavours from the veggies I chose and griddle fried, give off a very rustic and earthy flavour. For a super impressive culinary display, serve with a beetroot and red onion salad with my Lime Feta crumbled on top (see recipe pg 67), or some toasted pine nuts, with a dressing of olive oil and freshly squeezed lemon. Or you could serve with a cucumber, mint, spring onion salad, with olive oil and lemon dressing. The taste of this bake will blow you away . . .

---

2 courgettes/zucchini (I used the round marrow ones), sliced, griddle pan fried & then set aside
2 to 3 red Romano peppers, cut lengthways, griddle pan fried, and set aside
1 medium sized aubergine/ eggplant, cut lengthways, griddle pan fried, and set aside

Red Pepper Sauce

4 to 5 medium sized ripe tomatoes
2 cloves garlic
a drizzle of olive oil
salt to taste
1 Tbsp tomato puree/paste
1/8 cup (30 ml) water
¼ tsp ground chilli powder

'Feta Cheese' Sauce

½ cup my feta cheese - don't worry if it's a little less (see recipe pg 67)
½ tsp nutritional yeast
1 cup cashew nuts (pre-soaked)
salt to taste
1 cup (250 ml) water
a drizzle of olive oil

Bread Layers

2 to 3 large pita bread, or any other Middle Eastern flatbread, grilled and set aside.

Garnish

a drizzle of extra virgin olive oil
za'atar and sumac, for garnishing before baking.

Liquidize/process the ingredients for the red sauce until smooth, then pour into a saucepan and simmer gently for 40 minutes until it reduces and becomes a nice red/orange colour, and set aside.
Meanwhile, process Feta Cheese Sauce ingredients until rich and smooth.

For your bread layers, if using pita, separate the pockets to use a flat piece, grill until golden (don't over cook), then set aside.
One of the flatbreads can be cut into around 6 pieces by hand for the top layer of the bake.

Now preheat your oven to 400°F (200°C).
Pre-grease an oven pie dish. Then place one layer of the bread and distribute a quarter of the veggies in layers on top. Now add the same amount of the red pepper and tomato sauce.
Now place another flat bread on top, followed by a further quarter of the veggies (but not the red pepper sauce), and pour half the amount of feta white sauce on top.
Last layer of the flat bread, add remaining veggies on top, and use up the rest of the sauces, finishing off with pieces of the flat bread. Then sprinkle on the za'tar, sumac and olive oil - decorate the edges of the dish with the red peppers.
Bake in your hot oven for half an hour or until golden.

Serve after 10-15 minutes with a salad of your choice.

SERVES 4

My Middle Eastern Turkish Style Stuffed Cabbage Rolls

I have always loved all things stuffed - by that I mean stuffed veggies, stuffed pancakes, and so forth. The element of suspense every time you cut open the object of desire, particularly when it smells so wonderful, is such a fun treat at table. As is experimenting with different fillings. These are a masterpiece, and have an incredible texture, full of Middle Eastern promise. You can serve these with my Vegan Tzatziki (see recipe pg 71), and whatever else takes your fancy - perhaps some hot pita bread, or a salad with my Lime Feta Cheese (see pg 67) - Glorious !

You will need around 10 large cabbage leaves, washed, and cut off any bits of the stem that are too hard or dense. Pre-steam your leaves, and allow to cool down totally.

Filling

½ cup pre-cooked red quinoa
olive oil
4 mushrooms, chopped and pre-fried (add a little garlic granules if you wish)
½ cup bulgur wheat, pre-cooked and set aside
1 tsp curry powder
½ tsp cumin powder
¼ tsp ground cinnamon
1 heaped Tbsp tomato paste
3 Tbsp fresh parsley
½ cup pecan nuts, or ½ cup precooked puy lentils
1 small white onion
3 cloves garlic
1 Tbsp (15 ml) pomegranate molasses syrup
salt to taste

Sauce

2 cups fresh tomatoes, washed and processed in a food processor
olive oil
3 cloves garlic, chopped
2 Tbsp tomato puree/paste
2 bay leaves
¼ cup water
a little salt to taste
1 Tbsp (15 ml) pomegranate molasses syrup
fresh flat leaf parsley, chopped, for garnishing

First, start off by preparing your bulgur wheat by covering it with hot water in a bowl, and leaving until the water has absorbed – around 15-20 minutes. Meanwhile, start precooking your quinoa according to the packet instructions, and pre-frying your mushrooms in a little olive oil, with a few garlic granules, if you wish.

Then heat up some oil in a separate pan, and fry your spices for two minutes, before adding the tomato paste, mixing all the time.

Next, in a food processor, process the parsley, the nuts (or, if using lentils, add them in for the last 5 seconds so that you are not left with a mush), and the mushrooms, until all is broken down.

Now add this mixture into your pan with the garlic, onions, tomato paste and spices, and stir for a minute or so. Then stir in the bulgur wheat, and mix well. Pour on the pomegranate molasses syrup, and mix thoroughly so that the grain picks up the sauce and flavours. Add salt to taste, and leave the filling to cool down.

Now, add a dessert spoon of the filling into the centre of each cabbage leave, leaving a border of a quarter of an inch closest to you, roll the sides of the leaves inwards, and then roll away from you until you have a cabbage roll. Make the rest up in this way - you may have a little stuffing left, but I'm sure you'll eat it, as I did.

Sauce & Assembly

First, process the fresh tomatoes in your food processor.

Then fry your garlic, add the tomato puree/paste, and mix on a low heat for a minute or two, before adding the bay leaves. Now add the processed tomatoes, and simmer for 20 minutes, then add the water, and allow to simmer for a further 15 minutes.

Now stir in the molasses, and gently place the cabbage rolls into the sauce. Cover, and simmer on a low heat for a further 20 minutes, then uncover, and leave on heat for a further two minutes. Then allow 15 minutes cool down period, and garnish with finely chopped parsley.

SERVES 4

'Moroccan Magic' Tagine

This is a real all-year all-rounder, and can be enjoyed anytime. A rich tagine, with long-lingering flavours, that will bring each and every taste bud to life. I love the aroma that emerges from this, and, for me, the taste, flavours, texture and colours of this recipe, are a celebration of nature's elaborately kind gift to us, with all its wonderful vegetables, herbs and spices. And they all come together here to dance their dance – the result is something between a mild but full flavoured curry, and heavenly chutney, with a texture that stirs it one way and the other. A very exciting dish, and also a great treat for non-vegans who love a little spice. I recommend coupling this gem with my 'Moroccan Magic' Spicy Couscous *(see page 101).*

---

3 shallots
4 cloves garlic
½ tsp ground ginger
1 tsp cumin seeds
1 tsp coriander powder
½ tsp ground cardamom
4 sundried tomatoes, halved
4 Tbsp (60 ml) olive oil, plus extra for frying veggies
2 sweet potatoes, cut into one-inch squares (or thereabouts)
1 medium sized aubergine/ eggplant, cut into half-inch squares
½ tsp turmeric powder
1 cinnamon stick
3 bay leaves
1 Tbsp (15 ml) date syrup
salt to taste (taste before you add, in case it's salty enough with the sun dried tomatoes)
2 cups (500 ml) water, though you may well need more depending on the consistency you prefer - add it one cup at a time, stirring it in well

In a food processor, process the shallots, garlic, ginger, and spices (except the turmeric and cinnamon stick) with your olive oil, until you have a little paste. Then add the sundried tomatoes, and continue to pulse for a few seconds.

Next, drizzle olive oil into a large non-stick pan, and start frying your potatoes and aubergine. Turn around when these have turned golden, and repeat the process.

Now add the onion mix from the processor to the potatoes and eggplant, together with the cinnamon stick and the turmeric, and allow all this mixture to fry into the vegetables, so that all the spices and their flavours are released into the vegetables – a wonderful aroma will begin to emerge.

At this point preheat your oven to 340°F (170°C).

Add the remaining ingredients (except for the garnish), squeeze in the orange juice, and add the water one cup at a time, stirring in the second cup after 5 minutes. Cover the tagine, and place in your preheated oven for one hour.

When you open the lid, the aroma will be wonderful. Garnish with fresh coriander, and Enjoy !

SERVES 4

'Moroccan Magic' Spicy Couscous

Couscous is a staple in Tunisia, Algeria, Morocco, and Libya, and also popular throughout the Middle East, Sicily and especially in France. It is essentially steamed semolina, usually served with a stew of vegetables and sometimes with meat also – taking the place of rice or pasta as a base carbohydrate. I have produced several memorable couscous dishes over the years, and for this simple one I used whole-wheat couscous. You can use this as an accompaniment – I recommend serving it with my 'Moroccan Magic' Tagine (see page 99).

400g (14.1 oz) whole-wheat couscous
400 ml (14.1 fl oz) boiling water
knob of vegan butter (optional)
2 Tbsp (30 ml) olive oil
4 cloves garlic, each cut into 2 to 3 pieces
2 Tbsp tomato puree/paste
1 tsp harissa (Tunisian hot chilli sauce)
a pinch of salt
8 Tbsp (120 ml) water
orange segments, to serve as garnish
fresh flat-leaf parsley, for garnishing

Place the couscous in a heatproof glass or ceramic bowl (I used a medium sized tagine dish), and cover with the boiling water. Place a lid on top, and allow the couscous to absorb the water for around 6 minutes. If you wish, add a knob of vegan butter at this point.

Meanwhile, in a small non-stick saucepan, pour in the olive oil, and fry the garlic for a minute or so, but be careful not to burn it.

Next, add the tomato puree/paste, and harissa. Lower the heat, add the water, and allow to cook for 10 minutes, stirring so that it won't stick or burn. Add salt to taste.

You will be left with a thick sauce – don't be discouraged at the quantity, as this is highly concentrated.

Now remove lid from the couscous, and pour the sauce over it. Fluff up with a fork, and garnish with orange pieces and freshly chopped parsley.

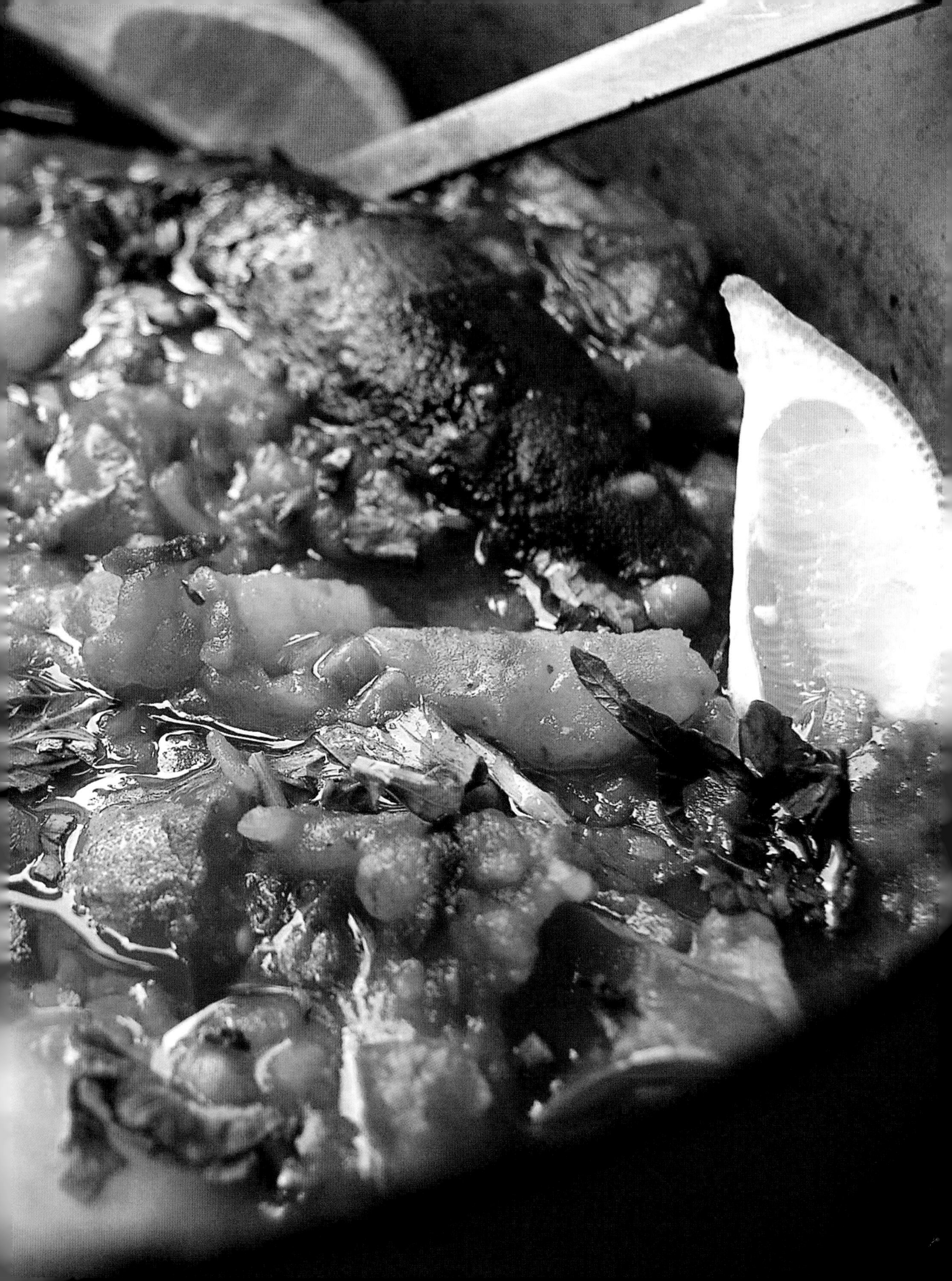

SERVES 4

Lemon Potato, Aubergine & Tomato Stew with Cinnamon

This stew is a combination of flavours, incorporating wonderful textures and aromas, and perfect for all year round, though I love it in the summer because of the edge from the lemon, which emanates beautifully from the potatoes, whilst the aubergine simply melts in your mouth. Serve with crunchy Mediterranean bread (I used my vegan butter on it), or if you want to keep it entirely gluten free, serve with short grain brown rice or any other gluten free grain of your choice. This particular recipe has Middle Eastern undertones, and an Indian touch - basically all the flavours that melt my taste-buds the moment I think of them. I have made variations of this in the past, though I have to say this seems to combine something from all my stews in one wonderful pot. An added bonus – it's also very easy to make.

extra virgin olive oil for frying
2 red onions, cut into fine rings (they will melt at the end)
4 to 6 cloves garlic – first punch or crush each clove, which makes it easier to peel (no need to chop)
2 large, or 3 medium sized potatoes, cut into wedges
1 medium sized aubergine/ eggplant, cut into wedges lengthways
1 bayleaf
1 cinnamon stick (don't omit this)
1¼ cups (315 ml) hot water
the juice of a large lemon
3 Tbsp tomato puree/paste
½ tsp asafoetida
½ tsp curry powder
4 to 5 fresh tomatoes (I use plum or zenguli for their higher solid content), cut into wedges
½ cup (65g) petit pois
1/3 tsp coriander seeds
sea salt to taste
¼ tsp turmeric powder
a sprinkle of aniseeds
a pinch of dried mint
1 lemon, cut into wedges - set aside for decoration
freshly chopped parsley, or coriander /cilantro, to garnish

First fry your onions in preheated olive oil, then add the garlic and the potatoes. Next, add the aubergine/eggplant wedges, and leave to fry on a medium heat for a few minutes, before adding the bayleaf and cinnamon stick.

Now in a large mug, add the water, lemon juice, tomato puree/paste, asafoetida, curry powder, and some more oil, and stir this well. Add the tomatoes to the stew, then slowly pour the liquid ingredients in.

Next, add your petit pois, and the remaining ingredients (except for your garnishing ones), cover, and allow to simmer for half an hour.

Mix gently, then either carry on cooking for a further hour on the top, or pop it in the oven for a mouthwatering effect – and be sure to taste for salt.

Serve with drizzled olive oil, and garnish with your parsley or coriander and lemon wedges.

SERVES 4

Exotic Orange, Aubergine & Okra Stew

I love stews, I have made a variety of them over the years, and if I had kept the recipe of each one, it would be another book in itself, full of magical ingredients. I apologize only for my non-conformist methods, but the result never disappoints, and well, I just love to go beyond the boundaries. This is a mixture of Iranian and Greek influences, with my own touch added on, resulting in a wonderful balance and contrast of taste and texture. Serve this with hot pita bread, and a salad of your choice - I served ours with my Fig Feast Salad (see pg 35), and well, we had just that - a feast - as I'm sure you will have also.

Marinade

1 lime, cut into wedges
6 Tbsp (90 ml) maple syrup
the juice of an orange, freshly squeezed

Marinade these together in a bowl before starting to cook your stew.

Stew

6 to 8 Tbsp olive oil (use less if you wish)
½ tsp coriander seeds
½ tsp za'atar (buy the dried herb mix – usually contains salt, thyme, oregano and marjoram, and sometimes sumac)
½ tsp turmeric powder
½ tsp ground cumin, or use the seeds
2 red chillies, slit lengthways
1 medium sized red onion, finely chopped
3 to 4 large cloves garlic, chopped (I cut mine julienne style)
4 Tbsp tomato puree/paste
1 large aubergine/eggplant, cut lengthways into slithers
2 cups of okra (I used giant ones) – also known as 'Ladies' Fingers'
½ cup (125 ml) water (more if needed)
1 orange, peeled and sliced into wheels
zest of a lime or lemon
1 large cinnamon stick
sea salt to taste
a handful of fresh coriander/ cilantro, chopped, for garnishing

First heat up your oil in a large pan for a minute, then fry the coriander seeds and the remaining spices for a minute until they release their magic.

Now add the onion and garlic combo, stirring them in well so that they incorporate with the spices, then add in your tomato puree/paste.

Once the onions have softened and become a little transparent, add the aubergine/eggplant, and stir well. You may need to add more oil at this point, as aubergines have a habit of drinking it all up. Allow them to start softening, and then add the okra.

Add the remaining ingredients, and let the sauce thicken and reduce. Be sure to taste for salt.

Finally, stir in the marinade mix, and leave to cook with lid on, on a low heat for a further 15 minutes or so. Make sure your sauce has thickened nicely, and that all the ingredients have nicely softened. The taste should be a perfect taste of sweet and savoury, with slightly bitter tones and a hot edge.

Serve in a preheated serving dish, and garnish with coriander.

SERVES 3-4

Sensual Runner Bean & Mushroom Stew

This is a simple to make stew - full of goodness, healthy, packed with flavours, and fused with a pomegranate molasses and hot chilli sauce. The texture is smooth, the mouthfeel sublime, the aroma wonderful, and the colours a work of art. A perfect Middle Eastern & Greek culinary marriage. Have I said enough ?

You can also use okra instead of runner beans if you like. Serve with your favourite bread, be it Greek bread, pita bread or any other of your choice. For a gluten free alternative, serve on a bed of rice.

extra virgin olive oil
1 white medium onion, chopped
3 to 4 cloves garlic, chopped
2 cups chestnut mushrooms, chopped
3 Tbsp (45 ml) tomato puree/paste
½ tsp ground cumin
1 tsp chilli sauce
a pinch of cinnamon, or a cinnamon stick
½ kg frozen fine runner beans (you can also use fresh - if so, slightly steam until a little soft)
2 Tbsp (30 ml) pomegranate molasses
sea salt to taste
1 cup (250 ml) water

Fry the onion in a large saucepan, then stir in the garlic. Add the mushrooms, and stir in until the mushrooms yield their juices. At this point, add the tomato puree/paste and spices, and stir until everything's nicely incorporated.

Now add the remaining ingredients, and cover. Allow to cook for around 20 minutes, checking on it periodically, and stirring to avoid sticking.

Uncover, and allow to thicken for a further 10 -15 minutes.

Ready to Serve . . .

SERVES 4

AROUND 10-12 TOMATOES

Tomato Dolmasi

I had a similar dish to this when I visited Turkey many years ago when I toured with my choir. In those days I was vegetarian, and was surprised to see the many vegetarian options offered in Istanbul. There was this small restaurant that many locals frequented, and this tomato dolmasi was served with their wonderful broad bean dip, and hot pita bread. I am serving mine with my own Lemon Drowned Potatoes (see recipe on pg 55). This is my take on the dish as I recall it, and I have made it several times over the years, and it keeps on getting better.

---

extra virgin olive oil
1 medium to large red onion, finely chopped
3 to 4 cloves garlic, chopped
¼ red bell pepper, chopped into small squares
1½ cups sliced, chopped mushrooms
1 tsp curry powder
¾ tsp ground cumin
1/8 tsp ground cinnamon
1 tsp agave syrup, or other sweetener of your choice
3 Tbsp sultanas, or giant raisins
the zest of a lemon
salt to taste (I use Himalayan salt)
1 cup pre-cooked quinoa - follow directions on pack, and when cooked, rinse under cold water, drain, and set aside
4 Tbsp toasted pine nuts or crushed walnuts
10-12 medium sized tomatoes (mine came off the vine)

a handful of fresh coriander/ cilantro, chopped

First, precook your quinoa, according to the packet instructions.

Then fry your onion until transparent, then add in your garlic, and fry for a further minute or two, but don't let your garlic brown.

Next, add in your chopped pepper, the mushrooms, the curry and the rest of the spices, and continue to fry, stirring intermittently to ensure even cooking.

Now add the agave or other sweetener, and then the raisins/sultanas, and the lemon zest.

Next, add the remaining ingredients (except for the fresh coriander, which should be added at the end, and the tomatoes). Mix well, cover for 2 minutes, stirring every now and then. Then taste for salt and sweetness, and adjust accordingly. Allow to cool down for 15 minutes.

Now pre-heat your oven to 350°F (180°C).

Then, having topped the tomatoes, use a teaspoon to fill each one with the stuffing, then place them in a large baking dish that you can cover. Drizzle with olive oil, add a pinch of salt, cover, and bake in your pre-heated oven for 1 hour, until the tomatoes are a little scorched on top. Then return to the oven uncovered for a further 10 minutes to finish off. Then straight to table, and serve.

SERVES 4-6

Zucchini & Lentil Moussaka

When I was out sourcing good veggies for this recipe, my green grocer told me that today was my lucky day – well, he knows I'm vegan, although he's not quite sure what that is, I think he thinks it's vegetarian. His eyes light up when he sees me, because he knows that my vegetables are 'my meat', and that I'm also a discerning customer. Today he had many large zucchini/courgettes, and he insisted I take a huge box of them home, and I mean huge, and for very little cost – "Have them for 2 Euros, Madam", "All right, I will" – and so I did. I'm rather glad I did, because I created the most amazing moussaka, using zucchini (courgettes) instead of aubergine/eggplant. Once I was going that green, I thought I should go all the way, and make this with lentils, instead of soya TVP, or the equivalent. I played with the flavours to create a truly delicious treat that works well all year round. This dish can be made a day ahead, and it will cut even better if so (remember to cut the portions whilst it's cold before warming it up). Serve with a vegan Greek salad, Enjoy with your favourite salad and Yasou !

Ingredients & Method for Layers

2 large unpeeled potatoes (or 4 to 6 medium sized ones), either boiled and allowed to cool, or microwaved until soft. When cooled, slice into 1/4 inch thick slices, and set aside.

4 very large zucchini/courgettes, sliced into 1/4 inch slices – fry in a griddle pan with olive oil until the griddle leaves its mark on both sides. Then place each one on absorbent paper - when you have fried them all, set them aside and allow them to cool down.

Cheese Sauce

1 cup vegan cheese (or 2 Tbsp nutritional yeast)
1 cup raw cashews, washed
1/2 tsp salt
garlic granules
1 1/2 cups (180 ml) water

Lentil Sauce

2 to 3 Tbsp (30-45 ml) extra virgin olive oil
1 medium sized red onion, finely chopped
2 cloves garlic, finely chopped
2 Tbsp tomato puree/paste
1 400g (250g drained) tin of lentils (drained) or use puy lentils – 1/2 a cup boiled until cooked, then drained
2 cups tinned tomato pulp
just under 1 Tbsp agave syrup, or other sweetener of your choice
3/4 tsp za'atar
2 inch cinnamon stick
3/4 tsp dried mint
salt to taste (about 1/2 tsp)

Garnish Topping

1 tsp za'atar
a drizzle of extra virgin olive oil

Cheese & Lentil Sauces

Place the cheese sauce ingredients in a high-speed food blender, and blend until smooth and creamy. Taste for seasoning, and set aside. Meanwhile, heat up your olive oil for the lentil sauce, and fry your onion until transparent. Then add your garlic, and within a minute stir in your tomato puree/paste. Now add the remaining ingredients one at a time, and mix. Then simmer gently for half an hour until the sauce reduces and you are left with a thick sauce to spoon into the dish – 20 minutes or so should do the trick, but if it needs longer don't deprive it.

Assembling

First, prepare a suitable oven dish – use a circular dish, so long as the dimensions are not less than 10 inches across and 4 to 5 inches deep. Now heat your oven to 350°F (180°C). Then place the slices of your pre-cooked zucchini /courgette at the base (you'll use up under half), being careful to cover the entire base, then add 1/4 of your red sauce scattered. Once again, add some zucchini slices, and cover with half your potato slices – spoon on half of the red sauce that's left, and then pour around half the cheese sauce on top. Using a sharp knife, make a few random holes. Next, add the remaining zucchini and potato slices, then the remaining tomato and lentil sauce, and finish off with the cheese sauce - try to distribute this around the middle and edges of the dish.
Finally, drizzle with the olive oil. Now bake for 30 minutes or until golden on top. Remove from the oven when golden, and then garnish with a little za'atar. Be sure to let it breathe for at least 15 minutes before cutting and serving.

Briam-Imam Bayildi

This recipe is inspired by my sister Androulla – who cooks wonderful Greek food, and is vegan herself now. This is my take on her recipe, and I think we may have just pushed it to the limit and taken it to another dimension.

Really this dish should be called 'Baked Veggies from Heaven'. They melt in your mouth, and leave behind them such magical flavours. Briam is a popular dish in Greece, cooked in the oven and often accompanied by the likes of tzatziki, olives and such like. Imam Bayildi is one of the most notable dishes to be found in Mediterranean cuisine, and also particularly in Turkish cuisine. Usually the dish consists of aubergine (eggplant), stuffed with onions, tomatoes and olive oil. It is also well known in Bulgaria, Israel, Greece, Albania and in Armenia by the Turkish name. It is generally known in the Arab world as imam bayouldi. The name supposedly derives from a tale of a Turkish imam, who swooned with pleasure at the flavour when presented with this dish by his wife, although other more humourous accounts suggest he fainted upon hearing the cost of the ingredients used to cook the dish.

A similar dish is popular in Iran, although other vegetables and herbs may also be added to the filling. I love it served hot with tzatziki and hot pita bread, or other fresh warm Mediterranean bread of your choice. Here is a fusion, and a dish to be proud to serve to guests – once the rich spices, tomatoes, and olive oil are massaged all over the vegetables, which are then covered in foil and cooked in the oven – that's when the magic begins, and the experience becomes heavenly. This will be a household favourite, believe you me.

I should add that briam is often cooked with far more oil than I have used – as much as a cup for the spice marinade alone. It does need oil, make no mistake – and Greek food would not be Greek food without it. However, I don't believe food needs to be swimming in oil, or that it's particularly good for you if it is. In this recipe I hope I've achieved a happy medium, but feel free to reduce the oil if you'd rather – I can't guarantee it'll taste the same though. And be sure to use a good quality extra virgin olive oil.

SERVES 4-6

2 large or 3 medium aubergines/ eggplants, peeled and cut lengthways (dip these completely in apple cider vinegar, so they don't soak up all the oil)
8 shallots - leave them whole
4 large courgettes/zucchini, cut lengthways
2 large sweet potatoes, peeled and cut lengthways
3 large Cyprus potatoes, or similar
4 to 5 Romano peppers, deseeded and cut lengthways
1 large onion, finely chopped
a few bay leaves
½ cup (125 ml) warm water

Spice Marinade
2 tsp ground vegetable stock, or bouillon
1 tsp Himalayan salt
1 tsp garam masala
1 tsp of harissa (I used a Moroccan rose harissa mix)
½ tsp fennel seeds
1 tsp coriander seeds
1 tsp isot chilli powder (available from Turkish stores)
6 Tbsp (90 ml) extra virgin olive oil

Tomato Marinade
660g tomato pulp
2 -3 Tbsp tomato puree /paste
½ tsp oregano or marjoram (I used fresh marjoram)
4 Tbsp (60 ml) extra virgin olive oil
1 tsp muscovado sugar
3 to 4 cloves garlic

Final Garnish (before the oven)
a handful of fresh marjoram or oregano, for sprinkling on top
the zest of a clementine, or other citrus fruit of your choice (marries so well with the cinnamon)
around 6 pieces of cinnamon bark – placed around the edges of the dish as well as in the centre

Having chopped and peeled the veggies above, including dipping the aubergine in vinegar, remove and place all the veggies and the bay leaves in a very large oven dish. Take this opportunity to preheat your oven to 350°F (180°C). Then massage in the spice marinade (see below), making sure that all of your veggies get their fair share of this spice rub.

Next, do the same with the tomato marinade, having mixed the ingredients in a bowl.

Now add the herb, citrus zest and cinnamon bark garnish on top, as per my picture. Then add half a cup of warm water on one corner of the dish, and holding the dish carefully, swerve it all around from side to side, making sure you have full coverage of the thickish liquid. Then cover with foil, and place in your preheated oven for around 1½ hours.

Take out of the oven, and check that the potatoes have softened, then uncover and leave in the oven for a further 20 minutes on 300°F (150°C) – this dish may need longer, depending on your oven. Once the veggies are soft, the dish is ready to serve.

Next page Briam-Imam Bayildi

SERVES 4

Middle Eastern Style Mixed Peppers & String Beans in a Spicy Orange, Pomegranate & Tomato Sauce

I had in mind to make this with okra, but I used young green beans instead. The textures, colours, taste and aroma of this dish are difficult to describe - but the word 'Heavenly' comes straight to mind and soul here. Sweet, spicy, savoury, a little salty, hot, a party in one's mouth with every mouthful, so succulent. Serve with my Middle Eastern Turkish Style Stuffed Cabbage Rolls (see recipe pg 97), and hot pita bread.

---

1 medium sized white onion
2 leeks, chopped
2 red chilli peppers deseeded
3 cloves garlic
1 tsp smoked paprika
½ tsp cumin powder or seeds
½ tsp coriander seeds
olive oil
2 Romano peppers (long Italian red peppers), cut lengthways and deseeded
6 small bell peppers (orange, yellow and red), cut lengthways and deseeded
2 Tbsp tomato puree/paste
salt to taste
the zest of 1 orange
1 tsp agave, or other sweetener of your choice
1 Tbsp pomegranate molasses
salt to taste
2 cups green beans or okra (frozen, but slightly thawed)
the juice of 2 oranges

First, process the onion, leeks, red chilli peppers and garlic in your food processor until very, very finely chopped.

Now dry fry the spices together for a couple of minutes, then pour in the olive oil, and allow it to heat up, but be careful not to let it burn.

Meanwhile, in a separate pan, fry the peppers on a high heat until slightly scorched, and remove onto a plate.

Add the tomato puree/paste, orange zest, pomegranate molasses, sweetener, and salt, and stir for a couple of minutes.

Next, add and the orange juice, and allow the sauce to cook for 10 minutes or so, before adding in the green beans and the cooked peppers. Cover for a further 10 minutes on a low heat.

Taste for salt, and allow the sauce to reduce a little - it may slightly caramelize, but it will taste fabulous. If it's slightly overcooked, just add a little water - but remember that whilst we're after a rich thick sauce, there should be enough to be able to enjoy with some bread.

Stuffed Romano Peppers

Most red peppers available in the supermarkets these days are just about edible – often sold in spectacularly colourful packs along with yellow and orange peppers, and all glasshouse grown. The plus side is they're not as bitter as their green counterparts, but the flip side is that they're full of water, and nothing like as flavoursome as the elongated Romano peppers. The Romano variety is a different ball game altogether, and wonderful for stuffing. We've been enormously fortunate to have virtually all year round access to these succulent gems whilst in Malta, as they grow them in Sicily, which is just across the water from us. This is a complete meal in itself – just toss up an accompanying green salad, and you're there. Or else, serve alongside a Greek salad and pita bread wedges - better still, go for the full experience and serve with roasted golden Cyprus potato wedges – try my Lemon Drowned Potatoes (see recipe pg 55). I won't go on any longer . . .

SERVES 4

1 tsp coriander seeds
1 tsp ground cumin
1 tsp curry powder
1 tsp crushed cardamon
1 tsp mint
1 tsp mixed spice
1 tsp cinnamon
2 Tbsp (30 ml) olive oil (adjust to your taste)
1 medium sized onion, chopped
2 cloves garlic, chopped
1½ cups vegan mince/crumble, or use ½ cup TVP soaked in the same amount of hot water, or 1 cup of pre-roasted chopped pecan nuts, or 1 cup of pre-cooked puy French lentils
a couple of bay leaves
1 Tbsp tomato puree/paste
1 tomato, chopped
salt to taste
1 cup basmati rice (first boil it for 7 minutes, then drain and set aside)
¼ cup red quinoa (pre-boiled and set aside)
3 Tbsp chopped fresh flat leaf parsley
1½ tsp sweetener of your choice (agave or stevia will do the job)
1 Tbsp fresh orange zest
5 Romano red peppers (more or less peppers according to size)

Sauce

¼ cup (60 ml) veg stock of your choice
1 cup (250 ml) passata (tomato puree made without the tomato seeds or skins)
2 Tbsp (30 ml) tomato paste
3 Tbsp (45 ml) olive oil
a pinch of salt
a bunch of fresh basil leaves

First preboil your rice and quinoa separately – your rice for seven minutes, drained and set aside, and your quinoa for around 15 minutes, well drained and set asise.
Meanwhile, dry-fry the spices, then add olive oil and your onion.
Next, add your garlic and stir around for a minute, then mix in the vegan mince / crumble (or the alternatives mentioned in the ingredients list above), and the bay leaves.
Now stir in the tomato puree/paste and the chopped tomato, lower the heat and allow to cook for 10 minutes.
Add the remaining ingredients (including the precooked rice and quinoa), but not the peppers, as you will be stuffing those soon – reduce to minimum heat.
Using a sharp knife, make a slit along the length of one of the peppers (see picture), remove the seeds from its inside, then, using a teaspoon, stuff the rice and crumble mixture into it until it is full. Repeat the same process until you have stuffed all your peppers (it' s not easy to say exactly how many peppers the mixture will fill, because sizes obviously vary. But if you are left with more stuffing, no problem, heat it up and either serve alongside the peppers once they are cooked, or else save for a separate meal).
Place the stuffed peppers on a large plate, and refrigerate until you've made the sauce (or you can even make the sauce a day ahead).

The Sauce

Place the ingredients in a saucepan and cook for half an hour until reduced.

Assembling & Stuffing the Peppers

Preheat your oven to 300ºF (150ºC).

Pour the sauce in the base of a medium-sized oven dish (mine was about 14 x 8 x 3 inches), then carefully place the peppers in the dish, drizzle some olive oil gently on top, and cover with foil. Place in the oven for one hour, then uncover, and cook for a further 15 minutes.

Garnish with basil, sit down at the table, and simply Enjoy the Heavenly taste and texture of this delightful dish !

SERVES 4-6

Spanking Spanakopita

Spanakopita is a traditional Greek Pie – both rich and delicious – stuffed with spinach, onions and 'feta cheese', as well as a herb filling, and encased beautifully within a flaky filo pastry - it makes it a very attractive and decadent dish to serve. Once your ingredients are on your kitchen worktop, it's a relatively easy dish to prepare.
Serve with a Greek salad, or a tomato and onion salad, with a hummus side dish (see my Spicy Hummus pg 33), for a more traditional and authentic Greek experience – oh, and don't forget the black olives.

---

olive oil for frying
1 large onion, finely chopped
3 cloves garlic, finely chopped
10 oz (285 g) frozen spinach, thawed and drained from its water (squeeze into your clean palms to do this) – you may use fresh spinach if you like
1 x 350g (12.35 oz) pack firm tofu, drained
3 Tbsp nutritional yeast
juice of ½ a lemon
1 heaped tsp cornstarch (cornflour)
salt to taste
1 tsp black pepper
¼ tsp dill
½ tsp dried oregano (optional)
½ tsp dried mint
pinch of nutmeg
½ cup of my 'feta' cheese (see recipe pg. 67)
1½ cups vegan cheese of your choice, grated (I use our own Midas cheese)
½ cup fresh parsley

Pastry
around 16-20 Filo sheets (thaw from frozen)
3 to 4 Tbsp melted margarine (and a pastry brush for brushing it on the filo sheets)

Lightly oil a square baking dish, and set aside. Meanwhile, heat the olive oil in a large skillet over a medium heat. Now sauté the onions and garlic, until soft and very lightly browned. Next, stir in the spinach, and continue to saute for around 3 minutes. Remove from heat and set aside to cool.

Now place your tofu in a medium sized bowl, and crumble half of it into small pieces (you can use a fork to do this). Then place the remaining tofu in a food processor, together with the rest of the ingredients (except for the freshly chopped parsley and your grated cheese), and whizz for a few seconds until smooth. Now pour this mixture in with your crumbled tofu. Add the spinach mixture in with the tofu, taste for salt and lemon, and add more of either if you want to. Now carefully fold in your 'feta' and grated cheese, and mix gently with a fork. Your filling is now ready to set aside.

Preheat oven to 400ºF (200ºC). Next, place a sheet of filo on the base of your oven dish, brush with the melted margarine, and repeat this process with around 5 more sheets. Don't worry about the overhang of the pastry, as this will be folded in as I describe later on.

Now spoon in your filling, and flatten gently with a spatula or the bottom of a spoon. Add the fresh parsley on top of this mixture, and drizzle with very little olive oil.
Fold the edges of the filo pastry on top of this (it will only cover some of the filling, but don't worry). Add the remaining filo pastry sheets on top of the filling, using the same process of brushing each one with margarine once it's laid on to the topping, and then when you have placed them all, cut the edges with a knife, or simply tuck the remaining filo overhang into itself. Place in your preheated oven for around 35 minutes or until it's golden. Do not overcook it !
Remove from oven, allow to cool for 15 minutes, before cutting into square portions.

SERVES 4-6

Spanakopita Tart

Spanakopita . . . I love this open pie, but here is a twist on the traditional recipe, well, my take on an alternative to the conventional one as we know it, just for a change ! This pie is easy to cut, and packed with flavour, with a great texture. Nutritious, and a perfect treat, served hot or cold with a tomato, onion and olive salad, drizzled with olive oil and lemon. It's also soya free, for those who can't take soya. The aroma is quite amazing, and I guarantee you're going to love it !

Base

You will need a 9″ pre-greased pie dish
250g shortcrust pastry (I used Jus-Rol)

Filling

1 1/8 cup presoaked cashew nuts
1¾ cups (438 ml) water - you may need a bit more if it remains too thick
1 Tbsp nutritional yeast
¾ tsp salt
a pinch of black pepper
an entire portion of my Lime Feta Cheese, cut into rough squares cheese (make same quantity as in recipe, see pg 67)
½ tsp dill
1/8 tsp kala namak (optional)
1 Tbsp egg replacer, or cornstarch
a handful of flat leaf parsley, roughly chopped
2 cups pre-cooked spinach, drained, and chopped (use frozen thawed if you wish)

For the Top

1 medium sized red onion, cut into slices

Roll your dough to fit your dish, making sure that you cover the sides of your pie dish, and cut off any extra dough with a blunt knife. Then refrigerate.

Preheat your oven to 375ºF (190ºC).

Next, in a food processor, blend your cashews and water until a cream is formed, then add the nutritional yeast, salt, pepper, the feta, dill, kala namak (if using), and the egg replacer or cornstarch. Blend until smooth, taste for salt.

Then add the parsley, and process for only a few seconds until integrated, but don't overdo it, we're just after small pieces.

Now take your pie dish out of the fridge, and distribute the spinach on the base, then carefully pour the thick mixture around it. Finally, add the onion rings on top.

Place the dish in your preheated oven, and bake until golden.

After removing from the oven, leave the pie to cool for at least 45 minutes before cutting. Best made at lunchtime, and served for dinner, or better still, the next day. Enjoy !

SERVES 4

Aubergine Feast

Aubergine / Eggplant Slices topped with Vegan Haloumi, Garlic, Apricots, Roasted Nuts & Quinoa

This creation came to me in stages, almost like preparing an art palette in readiness for its masterpiece. I love the combination of fruit and nuts, spices, zest, the sensual texture of cooked aubergine/eggplant, the apricots, and the flavour of roasted garlic, which surprisingly tastes creamy and not harsh (unlike its severe taste when raw). Serve with my Lemon Drenched Potatoes for a heavenly finish (see pg 55)! This is an easy dish to prepare, and ideal for impressing your non-vegan guests - who knows, maybe even altering their preemptive impression of vegan food. For menu purposes, you could also make my Vegan Taramasalata for starters (see pg 25), served with small hot pita wedges.

½ cup red quinoa, pre-cooked and drained (don't overcook it)
around 20 stewed dried apricots
¼ cup of my Vegan Haloumi (see pg 69), cut into small squares
extra virgin olive oil
2 medium aubergines/eggplants, sliced and fried (I used my griddle pan for this)
½ bulb of garlic, finely chopped
1 shallot, finely chopped
1 cup of pre-roasted, chopped pecan nuts, or use the equivalent in pine nuts
¼ tsp ground cumin
¼ tsp aniseeds
around 10 sun dried tomato halves, chopped
the zest of a lemon
sea salt to taste (do not omit)

halved garlic to spread around the dish (optional)
freshly chopped coriander/cilantro, to garnish
pomegranate seeds, to garnish

I would first salt or 'purge' your aubergines. This pulls out juices that carry bitter flavours, and also collapses the air pockets in the aubergine's sponge-like flesh.
Very simple to do. An hour or so before you start cooking, rub salt over your cut slices, and let them site in a colander for an hour. Moisture will start to come to the surface.

Rinse the aubergine slices thoroughly with clean water to remove the saltiness, and squeeze out as much of the moisture as you can with your hands. Then pat them dry using kitchen towel – the drier the better, as this will also reduce the grease.
Now cook your quinoa and stew your apricots in readiness. You will also need vegan cheese in hand – I would seriously recommend making my Haloumi, as I haven't come across a similar commercial vegan cheese to date.

Pre-fry your aubergines in olive oil, and then arrange them in a large dish in readiness for the filling (by all means set aside, and cover with foil in the meantime).

Heat some olive oil in a large saucepan, then fry your chopped garlic and onion, followed a minute later by the chopped pecans or pine nuts, and spices. Stir well, then add the chopped sundried tomatoes and lemon zest. Taste for salt, then add the apricots, and allow to cool for 10 minutes.

Preheat your oven to 355°F (180°C).
Spoon the mixture, including the garlic halves if using, onto the aubergine slices -- and bake covered in your preheated oven for 15-20 minutes. Remove from oven, and garnish with coriander, fresh pomegranate seeds, and lemon wedges. Enjoy!

SERVES 3-4

Crispy Golden Cheezy Zucchini Fritters

These are the most awesome fritters ever. Golden, crispy, 'cheesy', and flavoursome to the hilt. The zucchinis themselves were amongst the best I had ever tasted in my life, so I wanted to make something rather special, where the taste could be savoured and celebrated at the same time. Something Mediterranean, and full of flavour, which I would serve alongside locally grown, organic roast potatoes. So, having now conjured up an amazing appetite, all that was really needed was the juice of a fresh lemon, some sea salt and some ground pepper. Mmmmmm, the flavours – these are a 'must make again' number.

---

4 regular/medium zucchini/ courgettes (about 1¼lb, ½kg), shredded (I used my processor for this)
1 cup (250g) firm silken tofu
2 Tbsp all purpose flour
1 cup grated vegan cheese of your choice (I used our own MIDAS mozzarella)
salt to taste
2 Tbsp parsley, finely chopped
1 medium sized onion, finely chopped
¼ cup dried breadcrumbs
1 - 2 Tbsp nutritional yeast
olive oil for frying

First, shred your zucchini. Then process your tofu, flour, grated cheese, salt, parsley in your food processor, and taste for salt. Blend until a little smooth, but it must remain on the thick side, and a little chunky.

Meanwhile, place the remaining ingredients in a large bowl. Then spoon in the contents of your processor, and, using clean hands, give them a good mix, making sure that all gets well blended. It will feel thick because of the zucchini, but that's fine.

Heat up some oil in a non-stick pan, and with a large spoon, spoon in individual size portions and fry them - make them whatever size you desire.

Preheat your oven to 300°F (150°C).

Remove from the pan when they are golden on both sides, and transfer them to a grease-proof oven dish. Place them in your preheated oven for 15 minutes or so, and serve with a salad, and roast potatoes, if you wish.

Squeeze lemon on the lot, and Enjoy!

MAKES 6 BURGERS

Kibbeh Burgers in Hot Pita with a Garlic & Mint Yogurt Dressing

- ½ cup Bulgur wheat, soaked in a bowl of water for 15 minutes, then leave to fully drain for a further 15 minutes
- 2 red onions, finely chopped
- 1 tsp dried mint
- 1/8 tsp dried dill
- 1 tsp issot (chilli)
- 1 tsp sumac
- ¼ tsp cumin powder
- ¼ tsp ground coriander
- 1 tsp Himalayan salt
- 2 Tbsp chopped pecan nuts, or toasted pine nuts
- 6 large sun-dried tomato halves
- 1 cup fresh flat-leaf parsley, finely chopped
- 1 tsp garlic granules
- 1 Tbsp flaxseeds (golden linseed – cracked, not crushed or ground)
- 300g (10½ oz) vegan mince/ crumble, soya protein (TVP), or 1 cup precooked puy lentils, pre-drained
- ¾ tsp guar gum
- 1 tsp agave
- 1 Tbsp tahini
- the zest of a lemon
- 1 Tbsp plain white flour, for dusting
- 2 Tbsp (30 mL) olive oil
- juice of a small lemon

Yoghurt Dressing

- 1 cup of Greek Vegan Yogurt (see recipe page 65)
- ½ tsp garlic granules
- salt to taste
- around 1 Tbsp (15 mL) olive oil
- 1 tsp dried mint (or by all means use fresh)

Kibbeh - known in Cyprus as Koupes – is a national dish of many Middle Eastern countries, traditionally made of bulgur (cracked wheat), minced onions and finely ground lean beef, lamb, goat or camel meat with Middle Eastern spices (cinnamon, nutmeg, clove, allspice). This is my own take from a Lebanese kibbeh that I had in a restaurant many years ago - I cannot recall what the meat was, but I do remember the flavours and colours were beautiful. Now I have turned them into a burger that you can enjoy in hot pita bread - this is one of my favourite burgers ever, and I have been tweaking them for years. Here is my own secret recipe for you to enjoy, and I promise you, you will !

NOTE : If you choose to use lentils instead of crumble/mince, they will be quite soft, but should still work.

First, soak you bulgur wheat in a large bowl of water for 15 minutes. After draining it well for a further 15 minutes, place it in a large bowl. Now process your onions in your food processor (or chop them very small yourself), and place those in with the bulgur wheat. Add the dried herbs and salt to the mixture, and mix with a spoon.

Process your nuts in your food processor until they resemble bread crumbs, then add to your bulgur mixture. Do the same with the sun-dried tomatoes, and then process the parsley until chopped fine, adding both to your bulgur mixture. Add in the remaining ingredients to your mixture, and stir well with a fork.

Place the bulgur mix in the fridge for 20 minutes. Then add half the mixture to your food processor, and pulse for around 10 seconds, just to incorporate it, and to make patties you can handle. Then do the same with the other half of the mixture. If you are using pre-cooked lentils, 2 seconds in the processor will be enough, as you don't want to be left with a pate. Now place in the fridge again for an hour or so, then remove. With clean hands, form them into burgers, dust with flour, and then fry them in hot olive oil in a frying pan for around 4 minutes on each side until they are golden. Flip and repeat.

Remove gently onto a kitchen towel to remove any excess oil. Serve in pita bread with iceberg lettuce, a squeeze of fresh lemon juice, and a dollop of my yogurt dressing. To make this, place the ingredients into a serving bowl and mix well with a small fork or teaspoon.

SERVES 6

'Chicken' Souvlaki Kebabs

Souvlaki is a Greek speciality, traditionally made using small pieces of meat, and sometimes vegetables also, which are placed on a skewer, and grilled – in other words, kebabs. As a Greek Cypriot and authentic Greek, I was of course brought up with this kind of food around me. As I grew up, turning vegetarian in earlier adult life, and vegan in more recent years, I found myself becoming increasingly unable to accept the enormous quantities of meat consumed in my own cultural cuisine. And yet, I couldn't deny, I was still drawn to the flavours, the rich sauces and marinades, so, as with so many other dishes in this book, it was another mini milestone reached when I successfully recreated souvlakis – but this time, the ethical way !

During the summer months in Malta, I have frequently grilled these up on the BBQ and served them to various guests, mainly carnivores, who have merrily chomped away, assuring me that they were missing nothing as they ate these meatless kebabs. In fact, most have since started to substitute with vegan or veggie faux meats as a result, which warms my heart greatly.

---

3 cups of faux chicken cut into 1 inch squares
1 large red bell pepper, cut into squares
1 medium onion, cut into squares

Marinade
1 cup (250 mL) olive oil
the juice of 1 large lemon
salt to taste
2 cloves garlic, finely chopped
a handful of fresh rosemary, chopped, or 1 tsp dried
1 tsp oregano

Place the marinade ingredients in a high speed blender, and blend until smooth. Then place the faux chicken pieces in a bowl and pour over the marinade - massage it around the pieces, then place them in a plastic sealer bag, or else in a container with a lid. Marinate for several hours before barbequing or grilling.

Then arrange the pieces on a skewer starting with one piece of the 'chicken' followed by one piece of the onion and red pepper, and continue to alternate until your kebab stick is full. Then make the next. Your slouvakis are now ready for BBQing or grilling - be sure to turn them around as they cook. When they get some colour, they are ready (will only take a few minutes).

Serve with hot pita bread and a Greek Salad, using pieces of my Lime Feta Cheese (see recipe pg 67).

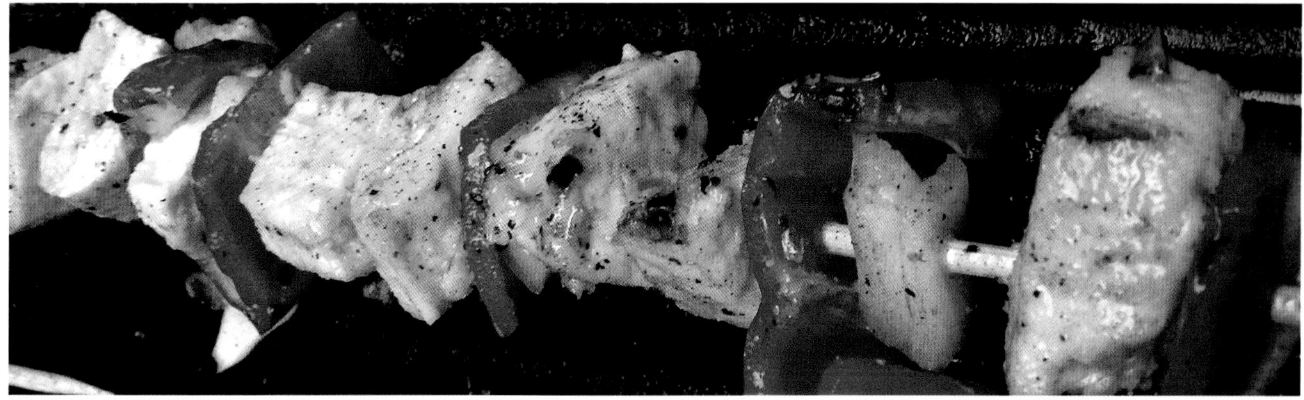

SERVES 4

Mouthwatering Vegan Keftedes (Greek Meatballs)

As a child, I would sit at the head of the kitchen table, and just watch my mother's hard working hands pinch out a handful of mixture that she would then roll into a meatball. I became mesmerized by how fast she could do this, and the wonderful aroma that the onion, mint and parsley emitted, together with the fresh, sharp smell of the lemon. I couldn't wait until she'd fried them, as that way I would get my teeth into them real fast. The problem was that once you bit into one, the experience would become instant 'savoury compulsion' - life just kept on getting better and better with my mother's keftedes every time.

These vegan keftedes I have created are absolutely divine, both in taste and texture – as for the aroma, it's heavenly. I am not going to say any more, other than enjoy the experience and savour it. I recommend you drench them in freshly squeezed lemon juice and serve with some creamy roast potatoes.

175g (6 oz) firm silken tofu, drained & cut into a few squares (I use organic non-GMO Mori-Nu)
1 red onion finely chopped
2 cloves garlic, finely chopped
2 Tbsp flat leaf parsley, finely chopped
2 cups ground vegan mince / crumble (use it from frozen), or use 1½ cups pecan nuts, crushed, mixed with ½ cup precooked puy lentils
1 Tbsp ground flaxseed
salt to taste (don't omit)
1 tsp curry powder
less than ¼ tsp ground cinnamon
less than ¼ tsp ground cumin
a few coriander seeds
¼ tsp dried mint
2 slices brown bread, wet and well wrung
1 Tbsp nutritional yeast
1 Tbsp (15 ml) fresh lemon juice
1 tsp lemon zest (optional)
plain white flour, for dusting
olive oil, for frying

Place all the ingredients in a large bowl, and with clean hands mash them together, so that you are left with a nicely blended mix (it will smell divine).
Next, dust a tray with flour, and then wet your hands lightly, and roll the mixture into as many balls as you can – I suggest not larger than an inch each in diameter.

Heat your oil in a non-stick pan - they can be deep fried (and would do well), but for health reasons it's better to shallow fry them, until lightly golden.

Place on a greased glass or ceramic baking tray, and bake in a hot 400°F (200°C) oven for 20 minutes. Serve and Enjoy !

SERVES 4

Keftedes with Spaghetti in a Rich Middle Eastern Sauce

And who doesn't love 'meatballs' with spaghetti, right ? And these Middle Eastern ones are just great. Loved by all, they make an excellent treat and add festive cheer at the table, any time of year. I have made these with a wonderful sauce that marries well with any pasta of your choice - spaghetti being a fun pasta to roll around one's fork, engaging in all the anticipation of mouthful after mouthful of intense taste, pleasure and umami. This sauce is rich, and of course, mouthwatering too !

NOTE : The keftedes can be made a day ahead and refrigerated before using in this recipe *- see recipe page 133*

Sauce

extra virgin olive oil
2 cloves garlic, finely chopped
¼ tsp ground chilli
¼ tsp ground aniseed
½ tsp za'atar
3 Tbsp tomato puree/paste
1 Tbsp (15 ml) pomegranate syrup
1 tsp (5 ml) agave syrup
2 cups (500 ml) passata (tomato puree without the skins or seeds)
salt to taste - around 1 tsp or so

Heat your olive oil, then gently fry your garlic with the spices, before adding the tomato puree/paste, stirring it around with a wooden spoon.

Now add the remaining ingredients, except for the tomato passata, and allow the flavours to incorporate for around 5 minutes. Then add the passata, cover, and allow to simmer for 10 minutes. Uncover, and cook for a further 10 minutes, until the sauce is reduced and thickened, adding a little water if too thick, so as to reach the desired consistency.

Now place your keftedes in the sauce, cover again, and cook for a few minutes until they are well heated. Serve on top of pasta.

SERVES 3-4

Bean & Nut 'Scampi' Balls

Here are some bean and nut keftedes, which taste fantastic on salads - especially a Greek salad, or as a party finger food.

You can use practically any bean to make these. After you've fried them, when you first lift them from the pan, they will feel softish, but when they cool they come into their own and harden a little, which makes them great for dipping. Either squeeze lime or lemon on top of them, or dip them in your favourite mix – perhaps sweet chilli sauce, vegan mayonnaise, or dare I say it, ketchup.

NOTE : The key to a successful result with these keftedes is to not over-process them, so that they retain a good, dynamic mouthfeel.

---

2 slices of bread (make into breadcrumbs)
a bunch of fresh flat-leaf parsley
1 red onion, roughly chopped
¼ cup brazil nuts
½ cup salted, roasted peanuts
3 to 4 cloves garlic
1 x 400g (250g net) tin of cannellini beans
a squeeze of fresh lemon juice
a pinch of cumin
1 tsp kelp powder
salt to taste
a dash of agave
¼ cup golden breadcrumbs (orange coloured if possible – I used Paxo)
enough oil for frying (see below) – olive oil is more healthy, or else canola or vegetable oil, if you're in a pinch
lime wedges for serving

Place the bread in your food processor, and process until crumbs are formed. Remove and set aside. Now process the onions, parsley and nuts, then add the remaining ingredients and process.

Now spread a generous film of your golden breadcrumbs on a medium-sized plate. You will then need approximately 1 tablespoon of mixture for each ball. Using clean hands, first roll the tablespoon of mixture in the palms of your hands, and then gently roll it in the breadcrumbs, and set aside in a dish or plate. Repeat this process, until you've made all the mixture into balls.

Next, heat your oil up in a pan to around 350°F (150°C) for frying. If you're shallow frying, you can use a frying or skillet pan – around ¼" oil in the pan, or else a deep saucepan for deep-frying, and enough oil to comfortably cover all your balls. I prefer to deep-fry mine, as the oil seals the outside with a nice crispy crust, but allows the balls to remain succulent inside.

Once your keftedes have turned a deep golden colour, place them on a plate covered with absorbent kitchen paper, and serve immediately. A few squeezes of lime or lemon juice, and Heaven awaits !

SERVES 2

Crispy Fried 'Calamari' (Kalamarakia)

Prior to going vegan, I was in love with deep-fried calamari drenched in fresh lemon - a meal in itself, served with a Greek salad, or simply dipped in tzatziki (see recipe on pg 71). So, here I am using dried palm hearts with the centre removed, easy enough to make. I have seen many different ingredients being used instead of fish, and I think that this just hits the spot..

---

1 tin of hearts of palm (220g drained)

Beer &'Fishy' Batter & Marinade
4 Tbsp plain white flour
6 Tbsp (90 ml) beer (I used Heineken lager - vegan)
3 Tbsp (45 ml) 'fish' sauce (see recipe on pg 25)
1/8 tsp garlic granules

lemon wedges, for garnishing
fresh parsley, finely chopped, for garnishing

In a standard 400g tin you usually get around 4 palm heart stems - around an inch or so each in diameter. Using a sharp knife, you will need to cut them into around ½ – ¾ inch circles. Before removing the centres, carefully dry the circles out with a paper kitchen towel. Then place them in a medium sized bowl (do not throw the centres away, you can fry these separately, but don't serve them with the circles if you want an impressive looking dish).

Now make your batter/marinade by placing the ingredients in a food blender and blend till smooth. Your batter should resemble fresh cream in consistency, a little bit thick, but not stodgy. Now pour the mixture on top of the palm heart circles, and make sure they are all covered with the batter. Cover and place in fridge for an hour prior to deep frying them.

Heat up a small wok of oil and fry them in small batches until golden. Remove and place on kitchen paper towel to absorb any excess oil. Serve with the lemon wedges and parsley.

NOTE : If you are after a fishier flavour, add some kelp powder to the batter - 1/8 teaspoon. Also experiment with adding some ground chilli powder for a little exciting bite.

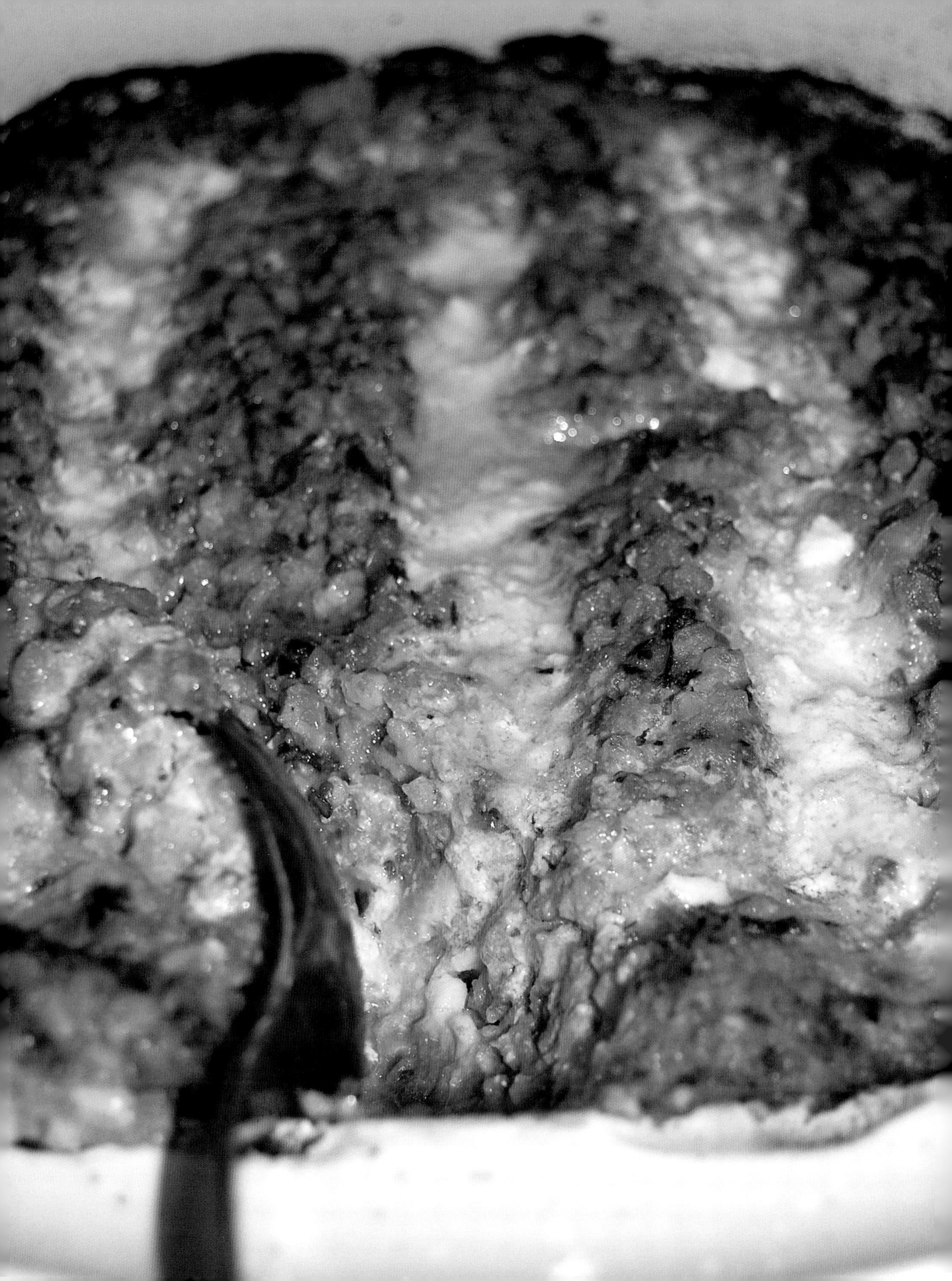

SERVES 4-6

Fresh Tomato Baked Rice with Greek Cheese & Spinach (Pilafi me Saltsa Domata)

250g short grain brown rice - precook until al dente, then rinse in cold water, drain and set aside
8 medium sized zenguli tomatoes, very roughly chopped
2 cloves fresh garlic, roughly chopped
salt to taste (don't omit)
extra virgin olive oil
1 cup of spinach (I used frozen and thawed it)
4 Tbsp grated vegan cheese - I use our own MIDAS Parmejano, or else use the recipe below
4 to 6 slices of vegan mozzarella cheese, or any other melting vegan cheese (I use our MIDAS mozzarella)
½ cup (125 ml) soya milk, or other unsweetened non-dairy milk

NOTE : If you're unable to find a vegan grated cheese, you can use :
1 cup raw cashews
½ cup nutritional yeast
1 tsp sea salt
½ tsp garlic granules or powder

Place the ingredients in your food processor, and process until it resembles grated cheese. Store in an airtight container in the fridge, where it will last for up to 2 weeks.

This dish is inspired by the wonderful 'Pilafi Me Tomatoes' that my dear mum used to make – and also reflecting the deep passion that I have for fresh tomatoes. Here embellished with wonderful slices of my own vegan Greek cheese wedged in between, as if to suggest a kind of rice baked fresh tomato pizza. I cannot describe well enough, or in any way do justice to how beautiful this dish is. All I heard around the table were my guests with their mouths full, expressing primal joy with their muted 'Mmmmmms' right up till the last spoonful. Always a reassuring sign when conversation dries up whilst the grub's on the table ! Enjoy with a simple green salad with olive oil and a drizzle of lemon. Heaven – Thank You God !

First, boil your rice until al dente, remove from heat, rinse in cold water, drain and set aside.
Then preheat your oven to 320°F (160°C).

Now, process the tomatoes, garlic, salt and olive oil in your food processor or blender.
Having placed your pre-cooked rice in a large bowl, pour the tomato pulp onto the rice, add the spinach and grated vegan cheese, and stir with a fork until the ingredients are all incorporated with one another.

Next, transfer your mixture to a medium-sized oven dish, and, using your fork, draw lines lengthways to create a trail about half an inch deep.

Place your cheese slices into the grooves you've created, drizzle on some olive oil, and place in your pre-heated oven for half an hour. Then remove from the oven, and pour the soya milk over the cheese wedges. Pierce some holes randomly around the dish - around 8 to 10 of them – to allow the soya milk to soak fully into the dish. Place your dish back in the oven, to give it time to turn golden, and get a bit 'well done' round the edges. Around 15-20 minutes should do the job (you may need to put the oven up a bit to achieve this – perhaps to around 320°F (160°C). I like mine a little on the well-done side, so I put it up to 390°F (200°C) for the last 5 minutes.

SERVES 4

Hot Tomatoed Orzo

This is a simple dish, but so very pleasant. Orzo is a pasta shaped like large grains of rice, it's versatile, and very easy to eat. The key to this being successful is to make sure it crisps at the sides and base when baking. The aroma is beautiful, and the taste is superb with its chilli kick, nicely set off with the sweetness of the tomatoes as they burst in your mouth, and then that little hint of 'cheese' to round it all up. A favourite 'easy recipe' of ours, and a dish that doesn't usually make it to the next day, as it's that moreish ! Serve with a crunchy green salad.

---

6 to 8 Tbsp (90ml to 120ml) extra virgin olive oil
3 large cloves garlic, cut lengthways
2 Tbsp tomato puree/paste
¼ tsp ground chilli (use more if you wish)
250g pre-cooked orzo pasta – follow cooking directions on packet
3 Tbsp vegan cheese (I used our MIDAS Parmejano – or see recipe pg 71)
salt to taste
around 14 cherry tomatoes (I used the long zenguli type), for garnishing
za'atar to sprinkle on top

Pre-heat your oven to 400°F (200°C).

In a frying pan, fry your garlic for only half a minute (don't burn it), then add the tomato puree/paste and mix well. Add the chilli powder, then lower the heat, and allow the tomato paste to cook for a further 5 minutes.
Now spoon in the orzo, mix well, add any vegan cheese of your choice, and salt - you may need to add a few spoonfuls of water at this point, and some more olive oil.

Spoon into a transparent Pyrex oven dish (or similar) – mine was around 7" in diameter and 3" deep - decorate with the cherry tomatoes, and sprinkle on the za'atar.

Bake for a half hour, or until the top is a little golden and the sides have crunched up - you can see this through the sides of your oven dish. If you have not yet reached this point, bake for a little longer, maybe a further 10 minutes or so. Enjoy !

SERVES 4-6

Pastitsio Perfetto

Pastitsio, sometimes spelt pastichio (or pasticcio in Italian), is a Greek and Mediterranean baked pasta dish, made with ground beef and béchamel sauce, with layers of pasta sandwiching the sauce. I have perfected the typical Greek flavour, with cinnamon, nutmeg & clove – and I defy anyone to spot that this is vegan in a blind tasting! Serve with a Greek salad and black olives.

500g (17½ oz) medium hollow macaroni
olive oil
1 large white onion, finely chopped
4 to 5 cloves garlic, finely chopped
2 Tbsp tomato puree/paste
454g (1 lb) ground vegan mince/ crumble or pre-cooked puy lentils
1 bayleaf
1½ tsp dried oregano
salt to taste (don't omit this - it's not a dessert)
ground black pepper to taste (don't overdo the pepper though)
a pinch of clove powder (don't omit)
6 fresh plum tomatoes, processed in a food processor
¾ cup (180 mL) hot water
1 cinnamon stick
2 tsp molasses or dark brown sugar

Béchamel
100g (3½ oz) margarine or any other vegan option
1 cup plain flour
2 Tbsp (30 mL) olive oil
¼ tsp nutmeg
2 cups vegan cheese of your choice, grated
700ml (24 fl oz) plain unsweetened soya milk

First, boil the pasta according to packet instructions. Then drain, rinse well in cold water, and set aside.
Meanwhile, process the plum tomatoes into a sauce in your food processor/blender. Then gently heat up your oil in a large non-stick pan, and fry your onion, mixing frequently. Add your garlic after a few minutes, and continue mixing. Lower the heat, and allow to cook for a further minute or so.
Next, add the tomato puree/paste, continue mixing, and then add your vegan ground mince, together with the spices, herbs, salt and pepper. Allow to cook for 5 minutes or so, until the aroma from the mix begins to emerge.
Now gently add the tomato pulp, and allow to simmer for 10 minutes, adding a little water at a time as it thickens. Add the cinnamon stick and brown sugar, cover, and cook for a further 25 minutes, stirring intermittently so that it won't stick.
Taste for salt, then leave the sauce on minimum for a further 10 minutes, whilst you make your béchamel sauce.

Béchamel Sauce
First, gently heat the margarine until it melts in a small heavy bottomed pan. Meanwhile, blend the remaining ingredients (except for the grated cheese) in your food processor.
Gently pour into the heated, buttered pan, mixing constantly until the white sauce begins to thicken. Then add the grated cheese, and continue to mix for a minute. Remove from heat once it has thickened. The trick with this sauce is to mix all the time, and taste it for salt.

Assembly
First mix in one ladle of the béchamel sauce to half of the pasta, then place this in a greased ovenproof dish, evening it out once you have done so. Next, gently spoon the ground mince sauce evenly over the pasta. Then add the remaining pasta, even out, and pour the remaining white béchamel sauce on top.
Place in a hot 400°F (200°C) oven for 45 minutes, until it has gone golden on top. Then drizzle on a little olive oil. Allow to stand for 15 minutes before serving.

SERVES 4-6

Aubergine Maqluba

Maqluba is a traditional dish of Jordan and Palestine, and is known as maklube in Turkey. Traditionally the dish includes meat, rice, and fried vegetables placed in a pot, which is then flipped upside down when served, hence the name maqluba, which translates literally as "upside-down". I decided to create my vegan version using pasta instead of rice on an aubergine/eggplant base, which looks absolutely spectacular when you flip it over to serve. Usually we toss up a simple green salad to accompany, since it's quite a filling and rich dish.

---

2 medium sized aubergines/ eggplants, sliced and pre-fried
300g macaroni, boiled to al dente
4 Tbsp (60 ml) olive oil
1 red onion, finely chopped
1 courgette/zucchini, finely chopped into squares
3 vegan sausages, slightly grilled, then processed into a crumble (I used Linda McCartney's, as they're reasonably neutral with a good texture)
1 cup frozen vegan mince / ground crumble
1 tsp curry powder
3 Tbsp tomato puree/paste
1 cup frozen petit pois
¾ cup (190 ml) water
½ tsp garlic granules
salt to taste
2 cups (227g) grated vegan cheese - don't omit (I used a mixture of my cheddar and my mozzarella)
1 cup (250 ml) soya milk or other dairy-free vegan milk (the creamier the better)
½ cup (125g) firm silken tofu (or 1 cup cashew nuts, processed with the vegan milk)
dry vegan cheese, grated (I used our MIDAS 'Parmejano'), or other brand of your choice

First 'purge' your aubergines an hour or so before you start cooking, by rubbing salt over your cut slices, and letting them sit in a colander for an hour. Moisture will start to come to the surface. Rinse the aubergine slices thoroughly with clean water to remove the saltiness, and squeeze out as much of the moisture as you can with your hands. Then pat them dry using kitchen towel – the drier the better, as this will also reduce the grease. Prepare your macaroni by heating a large saucepan full of water. When it reaches boiling point, throw in your pasta, follow the packet instructions, and cook till al dente. Drain, rinse in cold water, and set aside in a large saucepan or dish, in readiness for the sauce, which you will mix in with the pasta.

Whilst the pasta's cooking, heat half your olive oil in a large frying pan, and fry the aubergine slices until golden on both sides, then remove from the pan and set aside. It's important that each slice makes contact with the pan base, so you will probably have to fry these in a few batches, replacing the cooked slices with raw ones one by one. Next, heat up the remaining oil in a large saucepan, and fry the onion and courgette until lightly golden. Then add the processed 'sausage' mince, and the vegan mince, stirring them into the vegetables. Add the curry powder, and continue lightly stirring for a few minutes to blend in the spice, and to ensure that your mix doesn't stick. Next, spoon in the tomato puree/ paste, stirring continuously, and add the petit pois. Add in the water a little at a time, and add the garlic granules and salt to taste. Cover and simmer for 20 minutes until a rich thick sauce has formed (similar to a bolognese) - if you need a little bit more water, add it, but it must be a little thick.

Preheat your oven to 400°F (200°C). Meanwhile, process the milk, tofu and cheese in a processor until you have the consistency of single cream. Set aside for a minute. Now pour the sauce onto the pasta, and mix well with a wooden spoon. Add the tofu and cheese mixture you have processed (if using cashew nuts, add the nuts mixture with the cheese and milk that you have processed into one mixture) - pour this into the pasta dish, and stir it in well but gently. This baby is now ready for the oven. Next, grease an oven dish, carefully spoon/pour the pasta into the dish, and bake until golden on top and crusty at the edges.

Sprinkle grated vegan parmesan across the top, or other grated vegan cheese of your choice, and 'Abracadabra Maqluba' .... Flip it over onto a serving plate, and you should have a feast for the eyes !

SERVES 4

Epic Black Quinoa & Super Spicy Bolognese

This is probably one of the best Bolognese sauces I have ever made or tasted. Did I mention I have a complete addiction and passion for Bolognese ? And the reason is because I love to create many variations on this theme. We had had curry a few days before, and the urge for more spice (without excess heat) just brought out our love for it . . . in the midst of summer, believe it or not. It's such a treat. Check out the combination of spices that spun it for us. Luscious, stunning, full-flavoured, with great texture, this is easy to make, and a MUST for guests - vegan and non-vegans alike - the result is seriously impressive.

2 large cloves garlic
1 large white onion
olive oil for frying
3 Tbsp black quinoa, washed and drained
½ tsp smoked paprika
¼ tsp chilli powder
1 tsp panch puren (a blend of cumin, fennel, fenugreek, brown mustard seed and kalonji)
1 tsp coriander seeds
½ tsp curry powder
¼ tsp aniseed
3 Tbsp tomato puree/paste
2 cups (around 200g) vegan mince/crumble (you can use TVP, Gardein, Linda McCartney or the same amount of chopped pecans or puy lentils pre-cooked)
1 500g (17.5 oz) carton of passata (tomato puree without the skins or seeds)
1 cup (250 ml) good quality red wine (a must for this)
Himalayan salt to taste (I used just over 1 tsp)
2 tsp (10 ml) maple syrup or agave syrup
¼ cup (60 ml) water
2 medium sized potatoes, pre-cooked and cut into wedges (to be added to the sauce)
fresh coriander/cilantro, chopped, for garnishing

First, finely chop your garlic and onions in your food processor. Then heat up the oil in a large casserole, and fry the onion and garlic until transparent. Then add the quinoa, and mix through for a couple of minutes. Add all the spices, a little more oil, and let them infuse their magic for a couple of minutes more.

Add the tomato puree/paste, mix through for a minute, and add the faux mince of your choice – if you're using a frozen type, ensure it breaks down properly, then continue to stir for a couple of minutes.

Now add the remaining ingredients a little at a time, leaving the potatoes to the last 10 minutes. Taste for seasoning, and then allow to simmer for a good half an hour on a low heat.

Uncover, but keep an eye open so it won't stick to the bottom of the pan. If you prefer, you could bake the sauce at this point to save you having to watch over it. Either way, you should be left with a nice, rich, thick sauce.

Boil your pasta, add your sauce, garnish with fresh coriander, serve and Enjoy !

Place in a hot 400°F (200°C) oven for 45 minutes, until it has gone golden on top. Then drizzle on a little olive oil. Allow to stand for 15 minutes before serving.

Serve with a Greek salad, with black olives, and Enjoy !

opposite page *Bakdash ice-cream shop in the old souk in Damascus*

SWEETS

SERVES 4 TO 6
MAKES 1 LARGE RAMEKIN

Semi-Raw Coffee Crème Caramel

Ok, so this is not a typical Middle Eastern recipe, nor is it Greek in origin. But it's such a great sweet to impress your guests after one of my starters and mains, just to round things off nicely, and it takes things to another culinary dimension in one sitting. This is rich, incredibly creamy, exotic and memorable, and one of the best treats you could possibly serve. You can also burn a little cognac on it if you really want to push the boat out !

Caramel

1½ tsp instant coffee powder
¾ cup (188 ml) warm water
3 Tbsp muscovado sugar
a pinch of salt

Crème

1¼ cups + 2 Tbsp (345 ml) warm water
1 cup raw cashew nuts (see note)
1 cup (250 ml) pure coconut oil *
1½ Tbsp (22.5 ml) agave nectar
a pinch of turmeric
1 tsp vanilla extract

* Please look for a fair trade, cruelty-free brand of coconut oil

The Caramel

Stir all the ingredients in a small saucepan, gently heating until bubbles form on the surface - this will take some minutes, so be patient. Then pour the mixture into a medium sized ramekin dish. Now make the crème as below.

The Crème

First put the water into your high speed blender, add the other ingredients, process until smooth, then pour carefully over your ready caramel base.

Refrigerate and serve the next day.

NOTE : You will need to soak your cashew nuts in water overnight, then drain before blending. For this recipe you will also need a high speed blender.

SERVES 4 TO 6

Galaktoboureko (Greek Custard Slice)

This recipe of this wonderful galactoboureko is simply mouthwatering. I have been making this traditional Greek dessert for years now, and have perfected it 'down to a T'. So, if you love Greek food and Greek desserts, you're in for much delight here. Layers of filo (phyllo) pastry, creamy custard, and zesty syrup – not one for the weight-reducers, but an occasional treat and pick-me-up for sure !

Filling

175 g (6.2 oz) firm silken tofu (½ a 350g pack)
4 Tbsp custard powder (Birds Eye is our preferred brand)
2½ Tbsp semolina
4 cups (1l) soya milk, or other dairy free milk of your choice (must be creamy)
½ cup (125 ml) agave nectar
rind of ½ lemon (use a zester if you have one)
1 x 270 g (9.5 oz) pack vegan filo (phyllo) pastry - around 6 sheets (I used the Jus Rol brand)
melted vegan butter, or coconut oil, for brushing *

Topping/Syrup

¼ cup (63 ml) agave nectar, or maple syrup
1 Tbsp (15 mL) freshly squeezed lemon juice
¼ cup (50 mL) water
zest of 1 clementine / satsuma (optional), sprinkle on top
¼ tsp ground cinnamon, for dusting

* Please look for a fair trade, cruelty-free brand of coconut oil

Filling

Process the tofu and the rest of the ingredients (except for the milk and filo pastry of course) in your food processor for a few seconds. Next, add the milk, and process for 30 seconds.

Meanwhile, grease a 9 x 12 inch (or else 8 x 8 inch) oven dish, and line with around half the filo sheets, making sure the edges overlap the dish – trim with kitchen scissors if you need to. Then brush with melted vegan butter or coconut oil. Preheat your oven to 350°F (180°C).

Now pour in the milk custard mix, ensuring you pour it gently. Layer the remaining filo sheets on top of the custard mix, with butter brushed in between each sheet. Make sure that you join the edges of the pastry with the overlapping pastry from the base, so that they merge – it doesn't matter if there is still an overlap, as this adds both to the taste and texture, and the visual charm of it. Brush the remaining butter or oil on top, and place in your preheated oven for around 40 minutes, or until golden on top, and set inside.
Finally, pour the syrup on top of it, dust with cinnamon, and get ready for a great culinary sweet experience.

Allow to cool before serving - it tastes best when chilled.

Syrup

Place all the ingredients in a small saucepan, and heat gently whilst your pie is baking in the oven. Once the liquid has reduced, and become more of a syrup consistency, then it's ready for pouring on your pie.

SERVES MANY POLITE EATERS OR VERY FEW GANNETS

Kalo Prama

Recollections of my Greek Cypriot Auntie Maroulla's Kalo Prama (meaning 'Good Thing') makes my mouth water, and for good reason too. An incredible cook, always with a fridge and oven full of food, sweets & desserts, and always Kalo Prama when we visited. The smell of this cake is divine and rich, and for me full of sweet memories and magic. Not the healthiest of desserts, but scrumptious and delightful. I warn you this cake is very moreish, and high in calories, but it's one of those treats that's easy to make yet impressive to serve to guests, family and friends. The aroma and colours of this treat are simply a feast for the senses. An added bonus, with no eggs or dairy, it's great for the lactose intolerant, and of course it's completely cholesterol-free.

Cake

3 cups semolina flour
½ cup (125 ml) vegetable oil (you can use refined coconut oil if you wish *)
¾ cup caster sugar (or other dried sweetener of your choice)
1 cup (250 ml) vegan Greek yogurt
1/8 tsp vanilla crystals
1½ tsp bicarbonate of soda (the same as baking soda – but try to avoid baking powder, as this contains bicarbonate of soda, but also possibly various other non-vegan ingredients)
1 to 2 tsp (5 to 10 ml) rose water or orange blossom water
whole almonds, to decorate on top

Syrup

½ cup (125 ml) golden syrup
¾ cup (188 ml) water
¼ tsp ground cinnamon
the juice of 2 fresh oranges or lemons
the zest of an orange or a lemon (depending on which you use to juice)

* Please look for a fair trade, cruelty-free brand of coconut oil

The Cake

First preheat your oven to 325°F (160°C), and line a shallow dish (I used a 9½ by 12½ inch dish, around 1 inch high) with greaseproof paper.

Add the semolina and oil in a large mixing bowl, and mix thoroughly using a wooden spoon until incorporated. Next, add the sugar and the yoghurt, and mix well again. Add the remaining ingredients, and mix until you have a loose, but sticky, dough.

Spoon the mixture into your oven dish, and even it out with a spatula. Gently score the cake diagonally, just to make a mark, as per the picture, and sit a blanched almond in the middle of each piece.

Place in your pre-heated hot oven until golden, 15-20 minutes usually does the trick, but please keep an eye on it. When a toothpick comes out clean, your cake is ready. Allow a few minutes for it to cool down. Meanwhile, make your syrup whilst the cake is baking.

The Syrup

Place the ingredients in a saucepan and heat up for 10 minutes or so, or until it starts to gently bubble – be sure to mix it so that the ingredients emulsify well together. Then pour a quarter of the liquid onto the cake, distributing as best you can, and allow the liquid to seep through the cake for a few minutes. Then continue to do the same again until all the sweet liquid is used up.

Allow to cool down, and serve with tea, or as you wish (it's great with ice cream too). Be sure to store in the fridge though. An authentic Greek treat – what could be better to warm the spirits ?

SERVES 12

Turkish Halva

When I visited Istanbul years ago, one of the things that intrigued me the most was all the different shapes, sizes and flavours of halva on display. I've loved halva since I can remember, although my first taste was in Malta as a child. The minute it touched my lips, I fell in love. I am a huge fan of this magical sweet. I have created my very own halva now, with my own favourite flavour and texture, which I must confess (although with a great deal of modesty) I am very proud of. I am totally satisfied with this, and hope you enjoy it too. Try using other nuts such as roasted hazelnuts and roasted pecans from time to time. I forgot to say that although this version is reasonably healthy, it's also quite calorific - but that said, a little goes a very long way. Just make sure it doesn't go a long way around your waistline, so go easy whilst savouring every mouthful! This is an almost raw dessert.

Just over 1 cup (280g) light tahini - remove the oil from the surface in the jar
¾ cup (180 ml) either maple or agave syrup
1 cup (250 ml) coconut oil (I used refined pure coconut oil), melted *
¼ tsp salt
1 Tbsp (15 ml) rose water
½ tsp (2.5 ml) vanilla essence
¾ cup mixed nuts of your choice, I chose pistachio and roasted peanuts (yup, the salted variety)

* Please look for a fair trade, cruelty-free brand of coconut oil

You will need a small container - mine was a 5 x 5 inches square Tupperware.

Place all the ingredients, except for the nuts, in a food processor and process until smooth.

Then place half the mixed nuts at the bottom of your container. Then pour in the halva, and add in around 80% of the remaining nuts - mix them gently into your mixture using a chopstick or similar.

Garnish with the rest of the nuts, and refrigerate overnight. It should harden and cut beautifully!

SERVES 4

Middle Eastern Style Rice Pudding

'Roz bel laban', or rice pudding, is a very popular dessert in the Middle East, and although it is commonly served cold, it is sometimes served warm. My husband tells me that as a child he would often have rice pudding as a Sunday lunch dessert (with apple crumble, no less !) – but then, he is totally English, so what would you expect ! However, this version is definitely better served cold.

2 cups (500 mL) vegan milk (don't use a low fat milk, as you need a rich, creamy pudding)
½ cup (125 mL) water
½ cup raw cashew nuts (pre-soak them for an hour)
2 Tbsp sweetener (I used xylitol)
1 tsp vanilla extract
½ tsp finely crushed cardamom seeds
1 Tbsp vegan margarine or butter
2/3 cup short grain white rice (if you insist on using short grain brown rice, then you must cook it first and drain it - but I would use short grain white for best results in this particular pudding)

Syrup
1 tsp rose extract
2 Tbsp maple syrup

Or

1 Tbsp (15 ml) pomegranate molasses
1 Tbsp (15 ml) maple syrup

Extra
pomegranate seeds

Place all the ingredients (except for the rice) in your food processor - and whizz until you are left with a rich, smooth, cream-like consistency. Then pour into a non-stick pan, add the rice to your mixture, and heat up gently.

Allow the mixture to slowly come to the boil, then leave it to simmer, stirring often. When the liquid thickens, just stir in a little more milk. It is ready when the rice is totally cooked, and the mixture is thick, but not overly thick. I love mine somewhere in between.

For the syrup - just heat it up for a couple of minutes, and pour on top. Garnish with the pomegranate seeds.

Best-Ever Baklava

Baklava – a generic dessert from the former Ottoman Empire, but now served all around the world. This is a very rich sweet, and therefore one you are not likely to indulge in frequently. I make this once a year - maybe twice, at most. It's not totally healthy, and certainly not to be included in a weight-loss regime – but it is uplifting, and a dessert to enjoy and lift the spirits with. Having tasted different takes of this from several countries, I have created my own vegan version, and spiced it up with cinnamon, lemon and a few other wonderful ingredients. I have tried not to tamper with its original and traditional taste. For this reason, I have chosen not to sweeten it with date syrup, as this would then no longer be a baklava, but rather something richer and fruitier, which would steal the show from the fine, delicate taste of the filo layers, the lemon, and the spice. Also, I have not over-burdened it with too much filo – just enough to know it's there. Please just make it, and sit back and indulge !

TIP : DO NOT be tempted to eat this warm - it must be fully chilled to appreciate all its taste and flavour. Store in an airtight container for up to 2 weeks in your refrigerator.

SERVES 12 PORTIONS

Filling

1 cup roasted pecan nuts
½ cup mixed roasted nuts of your choice
1 cup raw pistachio nuts
a pinch of salt
1 tsp ground cinnamon
¼ tsp clove powder
½ cup brown sugar (I used molasses), or other dried sweetener of your choice
the zest of a lemon (optional)

Pastry

400 g (14 oz) filo/phyllo pastry (I used 1½ packs Jus-Rol, which is vegan. This gave me 9 sheets, each of which I cut into 2 pieces, so in total I had 18 pieces)
1 cup melted vegan butter/ margarine, or melted coconut oil if you prefer * - you will also need a pastry brush, for brushing on the melted butter or margarine

Syrup

1 cup (250 ml) maple syrup, or other liquid sweetener of your choice (e.g. agave syrup) - don't be shocked by the quantity !
1½ cups (375 ml) water
1 cinnamon stick
¼ tsp crushed cardamom pods (optional)
3 Tbsp (45 ml) freshly squeezed lemon juice
½ tsp neroli (orange blossom) or rose water

Place all the syrup ingredients in a small saucepan, and heat up gently until the mixture slightly thickens. This may take a few minutes - do not allow it to burn.

* Please look for a fair trade, cruelty-free brand of coconut oil

The Filling

Process the roasted nuts and the raw pistachios in a food processor until medium to small in size, not crushed into a powder. Then transfer the nuts into a large bowl, together with the other ingredients, and set aside.

Pastry & Assembly

Preheat your oven to 350°F (180°C), and grease an ovenproof dish approximately 9 x 9 inches.

Now carefully take one filo sheet, cut it in half and place it at the base of the dish - brush your melted vegan butter on top, then add the next filo half, and brush on melted butter in the same way. Now repeat this process, until you have 6 layers of filo at the bottom of your dish. Next, add half the filling mixture, and gently even it out on top of the pastry, taking care not to disturb the filo too much, as it's quite fragile.

Now repeat the first step, so that you now have the next 6 pieces on top of your aromatic nut filling, leaving 6 pieces to use on the top. At this point, using a sharp knife or skewer, gently pierce a dozen holes or so through the pastry (this will enable the syrup to seep through, when you pour it over the top later on after baking). Add the rest of the filling (although you may wish to leave a spoonful for garnishing, once it's baked).

Then repeat the first step to finish off, always greasing each slice of filo in between each and every layer – but don't pierce holes through this top layer. Now cut your unbaked baklava into either 9 or 12 portions (3 x 3, or 3 x 4), using a very sharp knife, and cutting very slowly as you do it. Wipe the knife with a clean wet cloth after each cut, so that you don't mess up the top layer with the filling.

Finally, just before baking, lightly sprinkle the top of the pastry with cold water. This will prevent the pastry from curling or over-hardening. Place in your preheated oven for 30-35 minutes, just until slightly golden - don't overcook this, as it won't work well if it's too crispy. Now, at this point, go and make your syrup (see below).

Remove from the oven, and gently cut around the edges of the pastry with a very sharp knife, to create the little space needed for the syrup to seep through. Now immediately pour on the syrup, evenly distributing it all over the top. Then allow to cool for a couple of hours out of the fridge, before placing it in the fridge for at least a further 4 hours. Serve and Enjoy !

SERVES 4-6

Pistachio and Ouzo Ice-Cream

The pistachio, a member of the cashew family, is a small tree indigenous to the eastern Mediterranean (Cyprus and Turkey to Israel and Syria), and Central Asia. Its seeds are a rich source of protein, dietary fiber, several dietary minerals and the B vitamins, thiamin and vitamin B6. Pistachios are also a good source of calcium, vitamin B5 and vitamin E.

At the Bakdash in Damascus (see picture pg xx), Syria, a pounded ice cream covered with pistachio called Booza is produced. It has an elastic texture made of mastic and sahlab, and is famous around the Arab World. Salep was a popular beverage in the former Ottoman Empire, and also in Germany and England, where it was known as saloop, and commonly consumed there before the introduction of tea and coffee in the 17th century. Tripoli's Al Mina district in Northern Syria is known for its Arabic ice cream including "ashta" with pistachios.

The wonderfully aromatic aniseed-flavoured aperitif ouzo is of course synonymous with Greece and Cyprus, and the halva I use here is the crumbly type made from tahini (sesame paste), which is a popular sweet throughout the Middle East, North Africa, and even into Asia and India. It is also perhaps one of the most nutritious whole foods sweets we can make, rich in protein, polyunsaturated fats, calcium, iron, magnesium, and plant sterols. So it seemed only fitting that a marriage of these three iconic ingredients should come together in the freezer with this delicious pistachio and ouzo vegan ice-cream !

250ml (9 fl oz) water
1 cup pre-soaked cashew nuts
350 ml (12¼ fl oz) soya milk or other creamy non-dairy milk (would probably also work well with rich coconut milk)
3 Tbsp (36g) sugar, stevia, or other sweetener of your choice
1 Tbsp (15 mL) melted coconut oil (organic refined is best) *
a few drops of vanilla essence
1/8 tsp of crushed cardamom or ground cardamom
2 Tbsp tahini
100g sesame halva, chopped (see Turkish Halva recipe pg 159)
a little citrus zest of your choice
2 Tbsp (30 mL) ouzo (for a non-alcoholic alternative, use 1 Tbsp (15 mL) lime juice instead
50g pistachio nuts, chopped (I processed mine)

* Please look for a fair trade, cruelty-free brand of coconut oil

---

Blend the water and cashew nuts first in a high speed blender. Next, add the soya (or other vegan milk) together with your sweetener, coconut oil, vanilla essence, cardamom and tahini, and whizz away until smooth. Taste for sweetness.

Now add the remaining ingredients (except for the pistachios), and pulse for 2-3 seconds, taste again, and adjust if you wish.

Pour into a plastic container, and freeze until solid (at least 4 to 6 hours).

Before serving, remove from the freezer for 15-20 minutes, scoop out and garnish with finely chopped pistachios.

SERVES 4

Rose Petal Ice Cream with Cardamom

I recall some years back in Istanbul having tasted rose ice cream garnished with pistachios and roses. This is dedicated to my recollection of it, and decorated with the Turkish delight that it had brought me. Here is a magical vegan version for you to enjoy !

½ cup raw pre-soaked cashews
1½ cups (375 ml) water
1 cup (250 ml) coconut oil *
2 drops rose extract
3 Tbsp (45 ml) agave nectar, or similar sweetener
a pinch of cardamom seeds
3 Tbsp (45 ml) rose syrup
a handful of pistachios, crushed
2 Tbsp rose buds (pre-soaked in hot water for an hour and separated)

* Please look for a fair trade, cruelty-free brand of coconut oil

Place your cashew nuts and water in a high speed blender, and process until smooth. then add half the coconut oil, the rose extract and a little at a time together with the sweetener. Now add the cardamom and the rose syrup and process again. Place the rose buds in hot water until they tenderize, and process the pistachios in a food processor and set them aside.

Gently pour the ice cream liquid into a small container (I used a square Tupperware 5¼ inches wide by 3 inches high), and freeze for around 3 hours. Then remove from the freezer, and swirl in a couple of tablespoons of rose syrup, to create a marbled effect – this is done once the ice cream begins to slightly thicken, so if you need more than 3 hours, give it longer.

Place back in the freezer, and once it has set, garnish on top with the rose buds and pistachios. Return to the freezer overnight, and your ice cream will be ready to scoop out and eat. If it's too hard, then allow a half hour thaw period before serving.

Index

C

D

E

F

G

H

K

L

M

N

O

P

Q

R

S

T

Miriam Sorrell

was born in London, but grew up on the small Mediterranean island of Malta. Her Greek Cypriot father owned restaurants in London, whilst her mother's background is a rich mixture of Greek, Turkish and Maltese, with family links throughout this region, including Constantinople and Athens.

Miriam is an international award-winning chef, and author of the best-selling 'Mouthwatering Vegan' cookbook (Random House 2013). She is a wholly committed ethical vegan, and has raised the bar in plant-based cuisine with her innovative creativity and constant striving to bring ever more delicious food to the vegan table. She has an innate understanding of how foods and ingredients interrelate, which enables her to quickly create a recipe in her mind's eye first, knowing the result in advance. She is therefore incredibly prolific and successful in her work, and always ready to encourage others around her and pass on her knowledge.

Miriam is also the creator of MIDAS Fine Art Cheeses, said to be some of the best plant-based cheeses in the world, and nominated for two international awards in 2015.

Miriam is a tireless campaigner for the rights of animals worldwide, and sees her work as an integral part in helping to reduce suffering by extending further the wonderful range of foods we can eat that contain no animal ingredients, thereby creating better health for us all, and granting back to our fellow inhabitants on this wonderful planet the right to live.

She lives in Malta with her husband, daughter, and their 5 cats.

Acknowledgements

I would like to thank my beloved daughter Zara for all her patience whilst I was making, creating and experimenting with recipes - and during the making of this book itself, that came to life a bit at a time, day after day. You cannot imagine how grateful I am for it, and for your taking some of my frustrated moments lightly !

Jonathan my partner, without you this book would not have materialized. Hours of research, editing, formatting, and high octane concentration and focus, as well as endless late nights into the early hours, has meant that this book we created together will bring about many a happy and satisfied vegan and non-vegan worldwide.

I am also grateful that I have created a feast of a book for all to enjoy, indulge, share and celebrate - to all you out there making these delightful wonders and creations, I wish you happiness in your kitchen and joyous results - in the spirit of joy I say to you YASOU ! X X X